Destiny

Books by Paul Harvey

REMEMBER THESE THINGS

AUTUMN OF LIBERTY

THE REST OF THE STORY *(1956)*

YOU SAID IT, PAUL HARVEY

Books by Paul Aurandt

PAUL HARVEY'S THE REST OF THE STORY

MORE OF PAUL HARVEY'S
THE REST OF THE STORY

DESTINY

DESTINY
by Paul Aurandt

From Paul Harvey's
THE REST OF THE STORY

EDITED AND COMPILED
BY LYNNE HARVEY

WILLIAM MORROW AND COMPANY, INC.
New York   1983

Library of Congress Catalog Card Number: 83-61567

ISBN: 0-688-02205-7

Printed in the United States of America

First Edition

1 2 3 4 5 6 7 8 9 10

BOOK DESIGN BY BERNARD SCHLEIFER

Contents

"Then bear me company in my far journey."
—EVERYMAN

1. The Blunder of the Body Snatchers

THE LAST DAYS of May 1878 comprised probably the most difficult time of John's life.

On the twentieth his friend, Augustus Devin, died of tuberculosis, "consumption," as it was called.

On the twenty-fifth, five days later, his seventy-three-year-old father passed away.

Daddy was to be buried on the twenty-ninth.

So there was John, standing quietly in this little cemetery in North Bend, Ohio. His father's burial service was just concluding. The whole family was there. And then John's brother, Ben, approached him.

Ben took John's arm and said, "Come with me."

The two brothers walked toward a nearby grave.

Ben pointed to the other grave and said to John, "Look what's happened!"

It was the grave of John's friend—Augustus Devin, nine days dead—and the grave had been robbed!

Augustus was gone!

In Ohio in the 1870s grave robbery was perhaps the most common crime. The ghouls were supplying medical schools with cadavers for dissection, so fresh graves were prime targets.

Brother Ben told John, "We're going to see to it that this does not happen to Daddy!"

Daddy's casket would be sealed in bricks and cement. The earth above would be filled with heavy stones. They would hire a watchman to check the grave every hour on the hour, every night for at least one week. They would do everything in their power to prevent those "monsters" from stealing Daddy!

The precautions were taken.

And then John started thinking about his friend, Augustus, and his heart ached. If he, John, had to turn every medical school in the state upside down, he would recover the body of his friend and return it to its rightful resting place.

Next day, May 30, John traveled to nearby Cincinnati, obtained search warrants, and began searching. His first stop, Ohio Medical College.

Administrative officials, stalling, suggested that John's friend may have been taken to another school in town. They had received no cadavers, they said.

John persisted, was finally admitted.

With the grudging cooperation of professors, he was shown classrooms and storerooms and laboratories. The body of his friend was nowhere.

But then, just as John was preparing to leave this college and search elsewhere, he saw, in the back of one room, a rope hanging taut from a windlass and leading down through a trapdoor in the floor.

John walked toward the rope.

Someone shouted, "No, wait!"

John pulled the rope, slowly and with all his might, and from the dark chamber beneath the floor arose a naked human corpse, suspended by a noose around its neck!

There was a cloth over the corpse's face.

John, with trembling hand, removed the makeshift veil to reveal—*not* the face of his friend, Augustus, but the face of his own father!

No one knows precisely how the grave robbers robbed the grave of John's daddy—how they eluded the watchman or penetrated the vault, or for that matter how they dispatched him so quickly to the Ohio Medical College. Of course, in that era of rampant cadaver trafficking, the grave robbers got plenty of practice.

Then, in 1881, the Ohio general assembly passed a law which put the ghouls out of business, a law permitting medical schools to use unclaimed corpses for instructive dissection.

It was public outcry over one incident more than any other which hastened that legislation, the widespread outrage over what had happened to the daddy of John and Ben, the senior *John Scott Harrison.*

For whether the body snatchers knew it or not, the body they pulled from that plot belonged to the only man history remembers as the son of one U.S. president and the father of another!

And now you know THE REST OF THE STORY.

2. Smile, You're Flying to Cuba

IT WAS TO BE a business trip for Al, yet it would have been a shame to leave his wife and their two small children up north in the winter chill while he enjoyed the Miami sun.

It was settled, then. Al's family would accompany him to Miami.

Monday morning, February 3, 1969.

Bags packed, Al and his brood arrived at Newark Airport. Out to the gate, to Eastern Airlines Flight 7. Takeoff.

One hour later aboard Flight 7, Al heard murmuring behind him in the cabin—growing louder. It was subdued yet intense, anxious, as though the passengers were becoming aware of something sinister.

They were.

Moments later a flight attendant passed. She was walking toward the cockpit. Behind her was a man, one of the passengers. He had a seven-inch knife blade pressed against the flight attendant's throat.

Al's face was instant cold sweat. He and his wife, stunned, stared.

They had read about the skyjackings, at least a dozen so far that year. Yet never had they imagined it happening to them!

A hushed hubbub of concerned conversation among the passengers. The flight attendant and the man holding the knife had disappeared into the cockpit.

Then, the captain's voice over the cabin speakers: "There is a man on board who wants to fly to Havana. We'd better go his way. Don't worry, everything is OK."

Silence.

Al heaved a sigh. In a calm half-whisper he reassured his wife. The captain was cooperating. Everything would be all right.

What happened next took Al completely by surprise. One by one, the ninety-some skyjacked passengers of Eastern Airlines Flight 7—began to laugh!

Their laughter was so hilarious that the skyjacker leaned out of the cockpit doorway to see why.

The passengers applauded.

The skyjacker was bewildered, utterly confounded. "What are you laughing at?" he demanded.

They laughed louder.

Al saw a Catholic priest, begged him to calm the passengers. The priest, already laughing, laughed louder.

Even *after* Flight 7 landed in Havana—even *after* the passengers were safely returned to the United States—the passengers were still taking the whole detour as a gigantic joke.

For at the outset of the trip someone aboard had recognized Al and informed the others.

Al had "cried wolf" too many times before. This, they were convinced, was just another of his pranks.

That is why the skyjacked passengers of Eastern Flight 7, February 3, 1969, laughed all the way to Cuba. Because they had recognized Al.

Allen Funt.

They believed they were on *Candid Camera.*

They were not.

It was a real skyjacker.

It was a real skyjacking.

The passengers just thought they knew . . .

THE REST OF THE STORY.

3. Freddie and the Duchess' Granddaughter

NOBODY LIKED FREDDIE. Or at least it seemed that way.

His own father detested him.

His own sister, Amelia, despised him.

His own mother said she wished a hundred times a day that he were dead. She, Freddie's mother, once called him "the greatest beast in the whole world!"

Nobody liked Freddie. Nobody who really knew him.

His home was the more merry England of two and a half centuries ago. Merriment was the one thing at which Freddie was good.

He lived lavishly. He did nothing for a living, relying entirely on an allowance from his father to finance his frivolity.

That allowance was fifty thousand pounds a year. An enormous amount of money, especially in the early eighteenth century. Still Freddie protested that it was insufficient for his purposes, that is, for his parties.

Therefore, young Freddie conceived a plan. He would marry a rich girl.

Freddie's father must have laughed. He remembered the awful hash that had come of his son's earlier engagement, a scandal the family had yet to live down. What woman of wealth in her right mind could possibly fall for Freddie?

Well, this is THE REST OF THE STORY.

Bold young Freddie sought and got an audience with the elderly Duchess of Marlborough. And he charmed the old girl. He presented himself as a dashing gentleman with excel-

lent prospects. Then he asked for the hand of the duchess'
favorite granddaughter.

Freddie could really pour on the charm when he wanted
to. Now, more than ever, he wanted to.

And he succeeded. He beguiled the elderly duchess into
believing his motives were purely romantic, and she granted
her permission. Freddie and her granddaughter would be
married at the earliest convenience.

What of the dowry, Freddie asked? According to custom,
the groom should receive a substantial dowry from a young
lady as highborn as the granddaughter of the Duchess of
Marlborough.

The duchess agreed. The dowry was set at one hundred
thousand pounds.

Freddie's financial worries were over.

One thing more, said Freddie. A small wedding would be
nice. A private wedding, even better. Best of all, however,
would be a secret wedding. To this also the duchess agreed.
The marriage ceremony would be held at her lodge in Wind-
sor Great Park—in secrecy.

Once more Freddie's motives were far from romantic. For
if his family or family friends were to discover what he was up
to, they would surely stop him.

They did, and they did. The marriage of Freddie and the
duchess' granddaughter was never to be. The highborn young
lady was spared for better things. She would marry another
and become the Duchess of Bedford.

And that is the way it happened *the first time.*

You see, Freddie was Frederick Louis, Prince of Wales,
heir to the throne of England more than 250 years ago.

And the favorite granddaughter of the Duchess of Marlborough, the beautiful young girl Frederick tried to marry for
her money, the fiancée who got away from the Prince of
Wales two and a half centuries ago.

Her name was *Lady Diana Spencer.*

4. The Little Car That Wasn't There

WHEN KEITH HAYES and his wife Cathy decided to adopt, they made up their minds that they would rear the adoptive young one precisely as though it were their own natural child.

She was only a day-old infant when her new mommy and daddy welcomed her into their Orange Park, Florida, home. They named her Viki.

Keith and Cathy loved little Viki as much as they would have loved their own flesh and blood. They adoringly dressed and fed and burped and cuddled and cared for her according to Dr. Spock. They agonized when she caught a cold. They rejoiced over the appearance of her first tooth. They bragged about her first step.

And toys! There were tricycles and dolls and balls and crayons . . . a mountain of playthings, many of which Viki was barely old enough to use or to appreciate.

So it was, in this environment of boundless affection, that Viki celebrated her infancy and toddlerhood. It was Cathy who first witnessed the puzzling behavior.

It began on one unseasonably warm, sunny afternoon in January. Little Viki was playing with a toy only she could see—a toy that wasn't there.

Old enough to walk, she was marching around the room, pulling a make-believe string attached to a make-believe pulltoy. Then Cathy smiled and called, "What are you doing, Viki?" Viki, who hadn't realized she was being watched, now obviously embarrassed, immediately stopped her pretend game.

That evening Cathy related what she had seen to her research-psychologist husband. Keith said Viki had apparently reached the "pulltoy stage," when everything with a string becomes a toy to drag around. It was the imaginary part that Keith found extraordinary.

"See if she does it again," he said.

Viki did it again—and again, and again. At first, only when she thought she was unobserved, and eventually, all day long, no matter who was watching!

After a while, there emerged a new dimension to Viki's game. She would pretend to "fish" with the little toy car, would cast it away and retrieve it by pulling hand over hand on the make-believe string.

On one occasion, as she was pulling the same invisible car across the floor, the invisible string became tangled in something. Viki tugged with all her might, yet could not free it.

"Mama!" she called out loudly. "Mama! Mama!" And Cathy came running to discover the matter.

Much to little Viki's joy, Cathy played along, untangling the nonexistent string in an elaborate pantomime. But as Viki happily raced off with her imaginary toy, Cathy wondered at the significance of this curious fantasy.

Predictably, Viki outgrew it. And one day the little car that wasn't there wasn't there anymore.

The significance of her behavior was this:

It was incredible enough that Keith and Cathy had taught Viki to speak a few words understandably. But never before had Keith Hayes heard of such sophisticated make-believe.

For Keith Hayes was a research psychologist at the Yerkes Laboratories of Primate Biology.

He knew better than anyone that nothing is more human than creativity or imagination.

And Viki—was a chimpanzee.

Quite apparently, Viki was able to conceptualize. But to what extent could she make conceptual distinctions? For the answer, Keith and Cathy devised a series of visual tests.

Viki's people-parents would attempt to communicate with her through pictures.

First they would see if she could distinguish between animate and inanimate objects. They showed her dozens of color photographs: some of people and monkeys and dogs and cats and birds and insects; others of chairs and tables and lamps—and even a few tricky objects in the inanimate group, such as clocks and automobiles which suggested movement. By demonstrating examples of each category to Viki, she was taught to place the photos of animate objects on one pile and the photos of inanimate objects on another pile.

In this test Viki scored extremely well, 85 percent. Of her six errors, three were pictures of insects.

The next test involved the categories, male and female, people only. The photographic subjects were all fully clothed, and both sexes were sometimes depicted wearing shorts and slacks. Youngsters and adults were used. Some pictures showed only heads, others merely facial features.

On her male-female exam, Viki scored as well as or better than many human children in identical experiments.

The little chimp also excelled in color-distinction tests. And in correlating shapes, and in comparing sizes. She became so adept at identifying two-dimensional representations that once, upon discovering the photograph of a wristwatch in a magazine, she put her ear to the crystal, obviously expecting the timepiece to tick!

I'm going to hesitate here.

With the domestication of any animal comes a responsibility. Perhaps none of us can appreciate the extent of that responsibility without knowing THE REST OF THE STORY.

For there was one categorical examination at which Viki was particularly proficient: the dissociation of photos of people and chimpanzees.

With different clothing and different poses and different camera angles, the test was made as difficult as possible.

Yet no matter how many times Viki took the humans-with-humans, chimpanzees-with-chimpanzees exam, she placed every picture correctly. With one exception.

Consistently, little Viki put photographs of *herself*—with those of the *humans*.

5. The Rescue of Mary Ellen Connolly

IN THE NEW YORK CITY of a century past, Etta Wheeler was a nurse and a church worker. She made rounds through the tenement houses, helping out when and however she could.

It was in 1873 that Mrs. Wheeler began hearing the stories.

Neighbors in one tenement house were certain something terrible was going on in the Connolly apartment. Every night they heard the screams of a small child. Would Mrs. Wheeler please look into it, the neighbors asked?

The reports were too disturbing to be ignored, and so one day Mrs. Wheeler knocked on the apartment door of Mr. Francis Connolly and his wife Mary.

Yes, they had a child, they said. A nine-year-old foster daughter named Mary Ellen. What of it?

Mrs. Wheeler talked herself inside and caught a glimpse of the unimaginable truth. The Connollys had chained their little girl to her bedpost. Her body was covered with wounds and welts and bruises in various stages of healing. She was emaciated from what could not have been more than a bread-and-water diet.

Seeing this, Mrs. Wheeler demanded that the child be turned over to her. The Connollys told the nurse to mind her own business and be on her way. For months thereafter Mrs. Wheeler returned to the Connolly apartment, hoping to rescue little Mary Ellen, and yet each time the door was slammed in her face.

Everywhere the nurse sought assistance in the matter,

she was refused. Charitable organizations insisted they were helpless unless the youngster could be brought to them legally. The police and the district attorney advised that they could do nothing until evidence was furnished that a crime had been committed. And in 1873 there were no laws against child abuse—only an unwritten law that parents could rear their children in whatever way they saw fit, even if that way were unspeakably brutal.

The "meddling" Mrs. Wheeler had one last hope: a gentleman named Henry Bergh. Mr. Bergh and the men serving under him comprised a law-enforcement agency. They were granted police power in New York City.

Early in 1874, Mrs. Wheeler visited this same Henry Bergh, described the ordeal of little Mary Ellen Connolly, and begged Bergh to intervene. Moved by what he had heard, Bergh immediately assigned two of his best officers to the case. They invaded the Connolly apartment and, armed with a writ of *habeas corpus,* took the cowering child into their protective custody.

Weak and hurting, whiplashed and scissor-slashed, the little girl had to be brought into the courtroom on a stretcher. Spectators, men and women alike, wept aloud. The judge himself had to turn away, so pitiful was Mary Ellen's appearance. There, in the middle of it all, was Henry Bergh, his voice filled with emotion as he recited the law which would save Mary Ellen and send her abusing mother to the penitentiary for one year.

A warm, loving home was found for the wretched little girl. It sounds almost like a fairy tale, but she really did live happily ever after.

And so did many others like her. For it was the case of Mary Ellen Connolly which inspired this nation's movement to protect defenseless children.

Even more specifically, that movement owes Henry Bergh. For when he rescued that battered child from a New

York tenement, he did so by the authority of the only extant law that applied.

Henry Bergh was founder and president of the ASPCA.

To save Mary Ellen's life, he had to state in court: "Your Honor, the child is an animal."

Now you know THE REST OF THE STORY.

6. Run for Your Life

ROD WAS ELEVEN YEARS YOUNG and running away from home. He had been trying for three years. Once he had even reached a nearby town. On that occasion, as always, his family had caught up with him and brought him back.

This time Rod had to succeed. He might never have a chance like this again.

He had run away enough to know it had to be done at night. So it was night. And an interminable stretch of dusty Nevada road lay before him beneath the black velvet and diamonds of the desert sky.

He thought of the other times. Of how they had come looking for him in the old pickup truck. Of how he had walked for a while and then hidden in a ditch for an hour or two, hoping his stepfather would be satisfied he was searching the wrong road.

His stepfather. He was the one Rod was trying to escape.

A big man. Dark, good-looking. Rugged from outdoor work grading highways for the WPA.

Had he been a mean man, Rod might have stuck it out, stuck around. Mean you can deal with sometimes. But Rod's stepfather, big Bill Hooper, had a sickness. The drinking sickness. And something worse. Something so dark and terrible that it could turn an otherwise compassionate man into a monster.

Out on that quiet Nevada road leading anywhere, the voices echoed, the cryptic memories played tag in the little boy's brain.

The town of Alamo. A two-story clapboard smothered in Virginia creeper and topped with a green tarpaper roof. The room Rod slept in, where peeling wallpaper revealed newspaper. A boy could learn to read pondering those walls, and Rod did.

Another memory: the sound of big Bill Hooper's footsteps on the front porch in the middle of the night. Heavy, stumbly, sluggish, they spoke without words. They told Rod his stepfather had been drinking and that in moments the boy would be dragged from bed and beaten.

Sometimes little Billy, his younger stepbrother, would awaken to Rod's screams and try to intervene. Often Rod's terrified mother would attempt to come between them. But nothing could stop big Bill once he got started. Nothing but merciful morning.

That's why a small boy began running for his life, always to be retrieved, occasionally with the aid of well-meaning strangers. "They all run away at his age," some said.

Now he was eleven. A veteran of the countless battles of the secret war.

In his young lifetime two arms broken, three ribs cracked, bruises and bashes from head to toe.

But this time when he got lost, he stayed lost.

An hour and a half walking. One hitched ride and then another. One hopped freight and a half-dozen more.

"Can you carry a surveyor's rod, boy?"

"Can you herd cattle, boy?"

"Can you cut trees, boy?"

"Can you dig a ditch, boy?"

And Rod could.

The road he had taken had taken him.

From the hurting.

Forever.

P.S. 1982's honorary chairman of the National Committee for the Prevention of Child Abuse was world-acclaimed poet and composer *Rod McKuen*.

Should someone ask you why, well, now you know THE REST OF THE STORY.

7. Whiff-Whaff

THEY WERE TWO of the most brilliant college football coaches who ever lived, and as turn-of-the-century contemporaries they were fervent, frequent sidelines rivals. Percy Haughton and Glenn Warner, whom friends and fans affectionately called "Pop."

Coach Haughton had a cold, hard, austere reputation. "Blood!" he often bellowed to his gridiron warriors. "That's what I want—blood!" He was also a supreme tactician who demanded precision, and it paid off in the record books. Three years of one four-year period, he made Harvard the nation's number-one team. Harvard's longest undefeated string—thirty-three consecutive wins—was engineered by Coach Haughton.

Pop Warner was a different sort; "creative" is an adjective often applied to his approach. During his years at Carlisle, the industrial school for American Indians, he became the country's best-known football coach. Forever developing eccentric formations and trick plays, he was recognized as the unmitigated master of razzle-dazzle. Pop was always searching the rule book for loopholes. He would try anything on the field that was not expressly forbidden.

Thus it was that these two dominant forces in college football, Haughton and Warner, were preparing to clash in the autumn of 1908, Haughton coaching Harvard, remember, and Pop Warner coaching Carlisle. Incidentally, this was the immortal Jim Thorpe's first full season as Carlisle's starting halfback.

Anyway, the week before the scheduled showdown of Haughton and Warner, Pop's team had pounded formidable Syracuse twelve-to-nothing. News of the shutout did not bother Coach Haughton until his chief assistant told him THE REST OF THE STORY.

Warner had won using an apparently unbeatable tactic. He had sewn a special padding onto the outside front of his players' jerseys—padding the precise color, size, and shape of a football. That meant a defensive player would look up after the snap and see what seemed to be a football in everyone's hands! Without knowing which player was cradling the real football, the Syracuse defense was utterly confounded.

To Harvard's Coach Haughton, such trickery was unsportsmanlike. "Whiff-whaff," he called it. To ensure a victory, Pop Warner had resorted to "whiff-whaff."

The night before the big Harvard-Carlisle contest Haughton actually approached Pop, asking whether he planned to use the trick jerseys for the next day's game. Warner smiled. "Nothing in the rules says we can't," Pop replied, and Haughton turned away. It seemed that Harvard had been defeated even before the first play.

Now—what to do?

It's only hours until game time. Not enough time to duplicate the deceitful device—sewing football look-alikes, which would be less effective on the dark-colored Harvard jerseys anyway.

But there was time for Harvard's Haughton to resolve this diabolical dilemma. And he did.

When tomorrow came the confident Carlisle players trotted onto the field, their brown football-shaped padding implanted elbow-high on their uniforms.

Of course, no team could get away with that today. In fact, it was Pop Warner's point-winning prank which inspired the rules prohibiting it. That is, Pop's prank—and Coach Haughton's retaliation.

For, despite the deviousness of their adversaries, Harvard won.

Before the game had begun, Haughton permitted Warner to choose a game ball from a sackful of footballs, all of which—each of which—Haughton had dyed crimson red. The identical color of Harvard's jerseys!

The ordinarily no-nonsense Harvard coach had produced his own hidden-ball play, his own brand of "whiff-whaff." And he had the last laugh, seventeen-to-nothing!

8. Herman

HERMAN WAS A Connecticut salesman. He sold everything from toasters to furniture, from vacuum cleaners to garages, anything that stood to make him a buck. He was always looking for the big score, the sale or the business deal that would set him up for life. He once even tried to invent a "revolutionary new method of refrigeration," but what he wound up with was a little box that did everything but get cold.

I'd like to acquaint you with Herman, if only because his breed is dying out. In some ways that extinction will be welcome. For Herman, simply put, was a bigot. He disliked and distrusted virtually anyone who was different from him, and that category encompassed a great many.

He never used the term "black" as it applied to people. He never said "Negro," which was quite a polite word in his day. To Herman, they were *"schwartzes."* He was always grumbling about the *"schwartzes."* Two insults for the price of one was irresistible to Herman. He often called his son "the laziest white kid I ever saw."

Women also had to be kept in their place. That attitude qualified Herman's wife Jeanette as a permanently oppressed minority. She could not speak up, and certainly never speak her mind, without risking Herman's gruff command to the contrary.

Thanks to Herman, the whole family lived at the top of its lungs and the ends of its nerves. It was a middle-class monarchy with Herman, the despot, presiding over all from his living room chair-throne. A red leather chair, Herman's alone.

No one dared be found in it when Herman was around.

One day the man who thought he had the world figured out outsmarted himself. The family was living near Boston at the time. Herman announced that he was making a business trip to Oklahoma and that if this one deal went through, he would retire a wealthy man. Herman never said exactly what the deal was.

He was arrested at the airport and charged with irregularities in the sale of bonds.

He was indicted, and he was convicted. He had been set up by men he had thought were his friends, and now he was taking the fall.

Herman's nine-year-old son would be twelve before Daddy was released from Deer Island federal prison. Thereafter, for all that had happened, so little had changed. Herman was still dogmatic in his opinions, critical, narrow, bigoted. Most remarkable of all, his little boy still found so much to love.

For Herman was a curious combination of things. No matter how insensitive he seemed at times, he was still affectionate. He seemed unreachable. Yet once in a while, if not often enough, Herman did reach out.

His son remembered it all, the bad and the good. And the boy grew up hating his father's bigotry and narrowness and dogmatism, while loving his father.

Herman's son became a television writer. And then a producer. And it was he who transformed a character from a British television series—who reconstructed that character in the image of his own father and shared him with the world—a believable, even lovable bigot who continually told his wife to "stifle," and who ruled his middle-class roost from a red-leather living room chair.

The television character who now seems so real—is Archie Bunker. But now you have met the man after whom Archie was modeled, Herman *Lear*. Of course you know his son *Norman*. Only now you know THE REST OF THE STORY.

9. The Herculaneum Dance Club

Dad wanted a son in his own image, so at birth the boy became a "junior." Henry Giessenbier, Jr.

As a result no one ever called him Henry. To distinguish him from his dad in conversation, family and friends called him Hy, and so shall we.

Hy Giessenbier was born on June 26, 1892, in Saint Louis, Missouri. He was one of six children.

The Giessenbiers were typical of most turn-of-the-century middle-income families in Saint Louis. They were never poor, although Hy dropped out of school in the eighth grade to work full-time.

He perpetuated his own education by reading a lot. Still in his teens, he grew interested in banking. As a young man getting started in the field, he often stayed at the bank until two or three in the morning, studying bookkeeping.

Hy was determined not to fall into the prevalent pattern: young man goes to work, goes nowhere fast.

It should be mentioned that by the time Hy was in his teens, Saint Louis was an old, basically conservative town. Then, for growing up in, it was a quiet town. Most youngsters were out of school and working by the age of fifteen, and often their first jobs were the jobs they died in five decades later.

Clearly, Hy Giessenbier was a rare exception to a virtually inviolate rule. For young, not well-educated Saint Louisans, there was practically no such thing as social or professional advancement.

If a young man were a go-getter, eager to succeed, he

would be lucky to work his way up to clerk by the age of thirty-five. By the time he had learned executive skills, he would be in his forties!

Hy did not consider this fair. Twelve signers of the Declaration of Independence were under thirty-five; Thomas Jefferson was only thirty-three when he wrote the original draft of the document!

So Hy Giessenbier—eighteen years younger—decided to do something positive for the young men of Saint Louis.

He started a dance club.

The Herculaneum Dance Club.

Obviously this seems frivolous considering Hy's lofty intentions, but if young people were to improve their prospects, they would first have to join forces socially.

Within a couple of years the Herculaneum Dance Club became the most popular such organization in the city. There were other dance clubs, of course, but none with Hy's high spirits and forward outlook.

In 1914 the Herculaneum Dance Club merged with six other socially minded groups to form the Federation of Dancing Clubs. Hy served as president.

The following year he expanded that organization into something called the Young Men's Progressive Civic Association. Within six months its membership had skyrocketed to 750 junior citizens. In fact, Junior Citizens was the group's next name.

And the members abbreviated that.

To "JCs."

That's right.

The Saint Louis dance club founded in 1910 by an eighteen-year-old eighth-grade dropout was the very beginning of an association that one day swept the world.

The Junior Citizens, who became the Junior Chamber of Commerce. At present, as half a century ago, they are called the *Jaycees*.

Now you know THE REST OF THE STORY.

10. Mysterious Benefactor

ONCE UPON A TIME, in the gentle foothills of America's Ozark Mountains, there lived a widow.

Her home was a humble farm cabin which she had shared with her husband, but now she was alone in the world.

One morning toward the hour of noon, three men rode on horseback into the farmyard. One of the men dismounted, knocked on the cabin door.

He explained to the widow that he and his friends were weary travelers, far from home, hungry and hankering for a hot home-cooked meal. Would it be too much trouble . . . that is, would she mind cooking such a meal for them?

The widow was reticent at first. Still, the strangers did appear hungry, and they were very polite. So she explained that there was not much food in the cabin, but they were welcome to what food she did have.

The men expressed their gratitude. Once inside the cabin, they were even more deeply touched by the widow's generosity.

It was obvious she was painfully poor. The little evidences of her lonely struggle to survive were everywhere: the meager furnishings, the supply cabinets mostly empty.

One of the travelers noticed a tear on the widow's cheek and asked what was the matter.

She replied that no one but she had eaten at that table since her husband's death. And now, having men in the cabin again . . . well, it just reminded her of happier times.

There was something else, and at this point the widow began to sob.

After four o'clock that very afternoon, she would be without a home. In less than four hours, the man who held the mortgage to her farm would come to foreclose. Eight hundred dollars remained on the mortgage, a hundred times more than she could afford to pay.

The travelers stared at each other in icy, ashamed silence. How could they have imposed upon a woman who was already heaped with such burdens?

When they finished their meal and had thanked the widow for her hospitality, the shadows of midafternoon were yawning in the farmyard.

One of the men clasped the widow's hand in parting. "You remind me so much of my own mother," he said. Into her other hand he gently placed a roll of bills. American currency.

Eight hundred dollars.

"When that man comes for his money, you get a receipt, now!"

Those were the last words the stranger spoke to her as he mounted his horse.

The widow watched him, smiling through incredulous, joyous tears, as he and his fellow travelers rode off down the dusty country road.

The story you have just read—that of the widow's mortgage and the generous stranger—occurred in the late 1870s in the foothills of the Ozark Mountains.

It is believed that single incident provided the factual basis for the scores of similar yet untrue stories that blossomed in its wake.

So as far as we know, it really happened only once. And this is THE REST OF THE STORY:

When the fellow who had held the mortgage on the widow's farm had departed the property, paid in full, carrying with him the mortgage money—he was robbed on the road in the woods nearby.

He was robbed of all the money on his person—by the same person who had given the widow the money! The "traveler." The stranger.

The mysterious benefactor: *Jesse James.*

11. Vice-president Who?

DID YOU HEAR the one about the two brothers? First brother went camping at Mount Saint Helens; the other brother became vice-president of the United States. And neither brother was ever heard from again!

That was supposed to be funny. And yet I have here a list of a great many men who would not have laughed: Daniel D. Tompkins, Richard M. Johnson, Charles W. Fairbanks, William Rufus DeVane King . . . each of them, at one time or another, only a heartbeat away from the presidency. And who today would even recognize their names?

A favorite 1980 television quiz show question: "Identify Walter Mondale." And the question recurred—because so frequently it was answered incorrectly!

Once upon a time, George Mifflin was our nation's vice-president. And George had a clear shot at the Top Spot. Yet, with a single gesture, he threw it all away.

Put yourself in George Mifflin's shoes.

Your biography so far, a politician's dream: respected Philadelphia family, Princeton education, mayor of Philadelphia, U.S. district attorney, U.S. senator—and now, in the mid-nineteenth century administration of James K. Polk, you, George Mifflin, are vice-president of the United States.

Already President Polk has announced that he will not seek a second term. Nothing stands between you and the Democratic presidential nomination. Why in the world would you cast it aside?

What happened was a split vote in the Senate over a tariff

bill that was getting a lot of national attention: twenty-seven senators for the legislation, twenty-seven against. As presiding officer of the Senate, George had to break the tie.

Oh, George knew what he was doing. He knew that if he voted in accordance with administration policy, he would lose the support of the states he needed to win the presidential nomination.

But George voted that way anyway.

And do you know that even his home state, Pennsylvania, turned against him? One moment he was a favorite son, the next they were hanging him in effigy. In fact, the response to George's Senate vote was so violent in his hometown, Philadelphia, that the Senate sergeant at arms was dispatched to that city to *rescue* George's family!

George received only three votes at his party's nominating convention in 1848. He then retired to private life, never again to hold public office. Aside from a brief foreign diplomatic service many years later, he passed quietly into the all-but-anonymous annals of vice-presidential obscurity.

He is long forgot.

But his name is not.

George became vice-president in the same year that Texas joined the Union. And the following year a handful of Texans got together and decided to name a teeny-tiny little village after George!

It was really no more than a settlement back then. In fact, it was so small that by the time George died, folks were just getting used to calling it a town.

George might have become president. Perhaps even a great one. Yet, mostly because of one silly Senate vote, he was lucky to get out of politics in one piece. And despite the obscurity of his vice-presidency, there is a plot of Texas real estate that will always belong to George Mifflin *Dallas*.

That is THE REST OF THE STORY.

12. *Anatomy of a Hypochondriac*

THIRTY-SEVEN YEARS YOUNG—too young to be dying—and yet the symptoms of terminal heart disease were unmistakable. She told friends that her life now "hung by a thread, which might snap at any moment."

And she went to bed.

And waited to die.

And did not.

Instead, she became an invalid, a fearful captive of the fatal symptoms that strangely refused to kill her. So many symptoms!—with but one source: psychoneurosis.

It was all in her mind.

This, then, is the anatomy of a hypochondriac.

The peculiar illnesses began when she was about seventeen. Her wealthy, socially ambitious parents had plans for her; she had her own plans, which included independence from her parents.

While I do not mean to suggest that the young lady was playing sick, it must be noted that virtually all her illnesses followed family arguments—as though sickness had become her subliminal defense against parental manipulation.

Age thirty-three she finally left home, got her own place to live, got happy. Her family frustrations gone, so fled her psychosomatic swooning.

This bliss lasted three years. For three years she was an achiever, a woman of responsibility and boundless energy whose only aches and pains were legitimate ones.

You, the investigator of her case history, must be alert at

this point, must watch for that moment at which she lapsed into her former self. She was thirty-six when it happened.

Palpitations, respiratory difficulty, sick at the sight of food. Within months she was bedridden, her pulse frighteningly rapid. There she stayed.

On occasion her condition grew suddenly worse, and the occasions were almost always predictable. Unwelcome visitors routinely inspired headaches and chest pains and gasping for breath. By now, apparently, her psychoneurosis had become a well-oiled problem-solving machine. She may even have understood it at one level or another, although outwardly she believed herself to be constantly at the brink of death.

Thirty-seven years old. Invalid. Anxiously awaiting the dread moment her heart would drop out from under her.

One day it did.

She was ninety.

Her illness really was psychosomatic, you see. For fifty-three years, more than a half-century, she lived in bed—for nothing.

True, her confinement accomplished certain things. It brought the people she wanted to her side, as her sudden attacks drove the unwanted away. Her bed even proved a comfortable vantage point from which she could observe and administer the work of others. Yet the psychoneurosis which held her prisoner for most of her life had deeper roots still.

Remember those three years during which she was not plagued by imaginary illnesses? Those years she had spent alleviating the suffering of others. Most of that time, at the Crimean War front.

For the passion her parents tried to suppress, a profession then regarded as unbecoming, was nursing. The young lady was happy only as an active nurse. Otherwise, she was a hopeless, helpless hypochondriac.

Yet so astonishing was her physical and emotional strength, her sheer endurance as a nurse during the Crimean

War, that nursing became a respectable occupation through her example.

The world forgot, or chose to ignore, that she spent the rest of her life—more than a half-century—in bed, in fear, in vain.

You know her as *Florence Nightingale.* Only now you know THE REST OF THE STORY.

13. Cubs' Curse

BY MID-BASEBALL SEASON 1945 there was magic in the air around Chicago's Wrigley Field. The Cubs were leading the league by three and a half games. They had a phenomenal pitching staff, headed by ace Hank Wyse. Then, on July 27, the club acquired yet another super pitcher, Hank Borowy, from the Yankees. Borowy's opening game for the Cubs was a shutout. It was a harbinger of spectacular things to come.

In the bleachers of Wrigley Field, cheering each home-game triumph, were the fans—and one fan in particular: a Chicago tavern owner named Bill Sianis. Even those who did not know Bill by name could identify him. To strangers he was simply "the fellow with the goat."

He brought his pet goat to each and every home game.

Spectators often asked Bill if the goat were a team mascot or something of the kind, and he would answer nothing of the kind. The goat was his pet, almost like a friend to him, and the animal was especially fond of baseball.

That seemed true enough. Before each game started, the goat would prance restlessly in the aisles, his eyes searching the stands for who knew what. But at the cry of "Play ball!" the goat's gaze would be fixed on the field. He would just sit there with his master, apparently engrossed in the activity of the athletes. Some said the animal would even bleat with delight whenever the crowd roared over an exciting play.

Then one day, in that incredible season of 1945, the Cubs won the pennant.

Chicago's National League team was in the World Series.

Because of wartime travel restrictions, the first three series games were scheduled to be played in Detroit, home of the American League champion Tigers, and the remaining games were to be played in Chicago.

The first game was a shutout: Cubs nine, Tigers nothing.

Detroit rallied in the second game, won four-to-one.

But then in the third game, Chicago pitcher Claude Passeau pitched the second one-hitter in World Series history, producing yet another Cub shutout, three-to-nothing. And the Cubs came home. Leading the series two-to-one, they would now play the remainder of the series in home-park Wrigley Field. How could they lose?

Well, I don't know if this answers the question. But what happened next is THE REST OF THE STORY.

When Bill Sianis and his goat arrived at Wrigley Field for game four of the 1945 World Series, they were apprised of a very recent regulation: *No Goats Allowed.*

Bill explained how his goat had relished the regular season, had rooted vigorously for the home team, and now to miss the conclusion of the World Series would be the greatest disappointment of the goat's life. But Bill's protests were summarily disregarded. The goat was out, and that was that.

And that was the origin of the Cubs' Curse.

Then and there, Bill Sianis declared that the Cubs would lose the series and would never win another pennant in Wrigley Field!

Two-to-one ahead and only home games left, the Cubs nevertheless lost the 1945 World Series.

Coincidence or curse, the Cubs until this time have never won another pennant.

14. The Ghosts of the Paris Boulevard

IN THE PHOTOGRAPHIC COLLECTION of the Bavarian National Museum in Munich, Germany, is a daguerreotype dated 1839. It was taken by Louis Daguerre himself, apparently from the highest window of a Paris building.

The scene is one of a beautiful boulevard stretching into the distance. On the sidewalk below, a man stands with one foot up on a bootblack's platform. A tiny, blurry image.

This is the first human figure ever photographed.

There is something else intriguing about this Paris cityscape. Something almost unearthly. Looking at the picture, one slowly becomes aware of it. Then one is haunted by the desire to learn THE REST OF THE STORY.

Louis Daguerre was an opera scenery painter with an unquenchable scientific curiosity. For many years he worked with photographic pioneer Niepce toward the perfection of so-called "heliographic" reproduction. After Neipce's death Daguerre continued to experiment, ultimately discovering the process that was to bear his name.

The early daguerreotype we've been discussing is entitled *Paris Boulevard.*

One appreciates the exquisite detail in the picture from that distance, even the brickwork in the buildings, the tilework on the roofs, the individual cobblestones in the street. In the windows across the way one sees the wooden mullions and muntins clearly defined. The pleats in the curtains are easily counted.

Yet, with the exception of that one tiny, lonely figure on

the corner, the entire boulevard, a half-mile or more plainly visible in the gleaming sunshine, is utterly devoid of life!

The shadows cast by the slender trees suggest that it is neither early morning nor late afternoon. The boulevard should be bustling with strollers and shoppers and horse-drawn carriages, delivery wagons, perhaps even romping dogs and children.

But no one, save that one man on the corner, is anywhere in this downtown Paris scene.

Pervading the ancient daguerreotype is an eerie calm, as though someone had just dropped the neutron bomb.

The glorious Paris daylight, praised as unique by generations of artists, shimmers everywhere, illuminating the intricacies of the ubiquitous lifeless objects. As we observe, we are convinced if there were life to be seen, we would see it.

Down through the ages it has been said in various ways that all around us is an unseen world. Many say they feel its presence; others claim to have parted the curtain and peered inside. The skeptics cling to a claim of their own: no camera ever lied.

So now it ought to be told.

That Paris boulevard photographed by Louis Daguerre was, during the moments the daguerreotype was taken, teaming with flesh-and-blood phantoms, people roaming the sidewalks, horses pulling carriages. And yet that early daguerreotype process was so slow that only stationary objects could be captured on the plate, like that one man patiently waiting for his boots to be brushed.

History honors him as the first man ever photographed, only because he was standing still!

15. The Voyage of Daisy's Bottle

PICTURE A BOTTLE. A whiskey bottle with air in its belly and a cork down its throat. A buoyant airtight bottle, bobbing in the Thames River at Old London Town.

Where will that bottle go? Ashore? Perhaps.

More likely, however, it will be swept out by the current into the Strait of Dover, and from there into the North Sea.

We are going to retrace the course of this sturdy glass vessel, a long and lonely voyage that really, actually took place.

Away from the east coast of England, northbound, past the Netherlands. Now, somewhere midway between Scotland and Denmark, still in the North Sea.

June of 1937 has passed into July.

The sealed bottle, urged ever northward by the ocean current, passes between Shetland Island and the coast of Norway. The vast expanse of the North Atlantic lies ahead, the Arctic Circle less than four hundred miles away.

The year 1937 bows gracefully to the next as the lonesome voyage continues. . . .

Hundreds of miles of Norwegian coastline is left behind as the intrepid bottle ventures into the icy Barents Sea. The northern coast of the Soviet Union is far below.

Years pass in those desolate waters, thaw and freeze and thaw again.

The currents lure gently eastward over Siberia, from the Kara Sea, past the "north islands" and Laptev Sea, and then through the East Siberian Sea.

And East meets West.

The bottle has remained intact and airtight for almost a decade now, as it floats into the Bering Strait between Siberia and Alaska on a southbound journey into the Bering Sea.

Then past the Aleutian Islands . . .

Then into the North Pacific . . .

Then along the west coast of the United States . . .

And now, at last, the restless voyage of almost twelve years and some twelve thousand miles has come to an end.

This course has been reconstructed by oceanographers. The path we've retraced is the one the bottle had to have gone after being released into the Thames.

But this is THE REST OF THE STORY.

It was a chilly day, March 16, 1949. A fellow named Jack Wurm was wandering a deserted San Francisco beach and happened upon that bottle, half-buried in the sand.

Jack, fifty-five, was jobless, near penniless, despondent. His restaurant business was bankrupt, his life savings gone.

Anyway, Jack discovered the bottle, saw something inside, broke the bottle on a rock and recovered the vessel's contents: a piece of paper, upon which was handwritten this message:

> To avoid all confusion, I leave my entire estate to the lucky person who finds this bottle and to my attorney, Barry Cohen, share and share alike. Daisy Alexander. June 20, 1937.

And yes, it did stand up in court, this "last will and testament" of Daisy Alexander, who had died in London in 1939. Daisy Alexander, who was the eccentric heiress to a large portion of the Singer sewing-machine fortune.

"Luck," she had secretly decreed, would determine her heir. And so Jack Wurm of San Francisco, broke and disheartened, down and almost out, was to harvest from a deserted beach—from a whiskey bottle that had begun its restless journey half a world away—*six million dollars.*

16. A Potion for the Plague

IT WAS THE MIDDLE of the night, and a French soldier was standing in the dark street, knocking at the door of a dry goods store, the Farina brothers' establishment.

By the way, this was a city in western Germany during the mid-eighteenth century. Wartime accounted for the presence of a French soldier. And the Farina brothers?

Both of them were named Johann: one, Johann Maria, and the other, Johann Baptist.

The brothers had come to Germany from Italy early in the century, had started selling silk goods in 1709.

Two decades passed.

The Farina brothers' enterprise grew.

By then Johann Maria had begun making a strange potion from a secret formula, and as a way of expanding the family business he had begun selling the potion. "Aqua Admirabilis," he called it.

Even after the brothers Farina had passed away, their dry goods business survived. And so did the secret formula.

So a French soldier was standing in the doorway of that same dry goods store in the middle of the night, banging on the door.

The proprietor, who was asleep in the back, groped his way through the darkness to answer the knock.

"What is it?" he asked the Frenchman. And the Frenchman, struggling with the German language, told the shopkeeper THE REST OF THE STORY.

Back in camp, one of his comrades was very ill. May even

be the Black Death. The soldier had heard, however, that a certain establishment in the city sold a potion for the plague, a remedy which rendered the mysterious malady harmless to those yet unaffected.

The proprietor nodded. The soldier had indeed come to the right establishment. There was a supply of the formula already mixed. The soldier could take it with him now, if he wished.

And he did.

For months to come, similar transactions would be conducted at the Farina brothers' shop. More French soldiers. Other foreign troops as well.

For those were the years of the Seven Years' War. One of history's more incredible conflicts, it eventually involved France and England and Russia and Prussia and Austria and Germany, even Spain and Sweden and Bohemia!

That city in western Germany was visited by a great many foreign troops, most of whom sooner or later were apprised of the Farina brothers' infection-fighting elixir. It was the French, however, who praised the antiplague formula most enthusiastically, and those French soldiers carried its reputation back with them to France.

As to whether the secret preparation was effective in combating any disease, who can say? Perhaps some of the ingredients proved lethal to some bacteria.

Fact is, what began as medicine survived the centuries as something else.

For this was one potion which future generations would consider undrinkable—yet no less effective.

And it was named after the city in western Germany where it was first concocted.

They used it to ward off the Black Death.

Today we still call it *eau de cologne.*

17. *See How She Runs*

Two ELEMENTARY-SCHOOL CHILDREN are running home from school. A boy and a girl, brother and sister.

But what's happening is more complicated than it seems. To the children this is a significant race, carefully planned, painfully prepared for.

What winning will mean to the winner is THE REST OF THE STORY.

If there were a track team, Eddie would be its star. But this is grammar school. Eddie is content to be generally recognized as fastest runner, grades one through six. He often races the other boys. He always finishes first.

Then one day he gets into an argument with his sister Jane, and the debate eventuates in a challenge. The little girl, momentarily forgetting her brother's recognized athletic prowess, declares, "Anything you can do, I can do better."

"Then race me," Eddie says. "I'll race you home right now!"

Knowing she is beaten before she has begun, yet too proud to back down, little Jane hesitates. All right, she says, they'll race from the front steps of school to the porch steps of home—one month from today.

Eddie's friends, who have gathered to listen, begin to laugh. Now she is trying to get out of it, they say.

No, Jane insists, she is not trying to get out of it. In one month, she will race her undeniably stronger, faster brother Eddie, and she will win!

That evening, Eddie begins feeling sorry for his sister.

She is just a girl, he reasons, and her idle boast can only end in humiliation. But it is too late to withdraw the challenge. Already Eddie's friends are eagerly anticipating the event. They are counting on him, so under no circumstances can he allow Jane to beat him.

Meanwhile, the little girl is preparing.

Each day for the next month, instead of walking to and from school, she runs. Everywhere she would ordinarily walk, she now runs.

Her stamina and endurance are improving. She is such a tiny tyke. Her short legs have to work so hard. Even with all this self-imposed training, she may still lose. But she will have given it her determined best.

Days become weeks. A month has passed. It's showdown day.

At the appointed hour after school, brother Eddie's many cheerers and Jane's comparatively few are assembled at the finish line.

They will race from the schoolhouse to the porch steps of the house on Kolmer Avenue, one mile.

They're off.

Someone down the block calls out, "Here they come!" Eddie is in the lead! Halfway home, he is still leading. Fifty yards to go. It seems now that surely he will win.

He will not.

For the brave little girl, the "sure loser" whose misfortune it was to take on the fastest boy in school, through the tedious improvement of her own endurance is still going strong when her competitor grows tired.

Asking for no advantage, she received none.

But she won.

Up for the race, against impossible odds, novice dedication versus established brawn, ahead only in the stretch—but the winner in the end. And three decades later, it would happen almost precisely that way, all over again.

For the recent history of the city of Chicago records that in

1979 a political upstart named Jane Byrne took on the Establishment with practically no chance of succeeding—and emerged Chicago's first-ever woman mayor.

Her remarkable triumph confounded almost everyone.

But then, the self-confident men of the media and the "machine" had never heard THE REST OF THE STORY.

18. Get Those Shoes!

MORE THAN A HUNDRED years ago the *Compiler* was a small but excellently published newspaper. Often its front-page news was days old, and yet for a provincial journal in Civil War times, it reported the nation's events remarkably promptly.

Reading the issue of June 29, 1863, one learns much about the era.

"The prospects of the Democratic Party were never brighter than they are at present," one article says. Republican Abe Lincoln was then president.

Some of the advertisements are fascinating. One, placed by Tyson Brothers, exclaims: "Eureka! Eureka! The Excelsior Washer is acknowledged by all who see it to be the most complete, and without exception, the most perfect Labor-Saving Washing Machine ever invented. Price $8."

Another ad, this one placed by the R. F. McIlheny store: "BOOTS AND SHOES comprising Men's fine calf boots, Men's Balmorals, Men's Wellington Boots, Congress Gaiters, Brogans."

It was this advertisement that attracted the attention of three Confederate generals, Ambrose Hill, Henry Heth, and Johnston Pettigrew. Hill was in charge of the entire Third Corps; Heth and Pettigrew were two division generals serving under him. The reason that one newspaper ad intrigued the Confederate brass was that much of the Third Corps, after many long months of fighting, was now marching barefoot.

They desperately needed footwear, and now they knew where to find it.

Heth told Pettigrew to muster his brigade, head for the town where the newspaper was published, and get those shoes. The town was some eight miles distant. Pettigrew and his men, about 2,400 infantry, started out in the early morning of the hot, humid thirtieth and returned late that afternoon. Where was the footgear, General Heth wanted to know? General Pettigrew related THE REST OF THE STORY.

On the outskirts of town he had seen a small group of Union cavalry; no infantry, although a few of his men had sworn they heard distant drums. With no cavalry of his own to perform reconnaissance, Pettigrew could only imagine the ultimate strength of the Union forces before him. He would not gamble with the lives of his troops. That's why he returned empty-handed. Sixteen sizzling, suffocating miles of barefoot marching—for nothing.

So Generals Heth and Pettigrew met with the commander of the Third Corps, General Hill. Hill told them to relax. Both he and General Lee were confident that the only Yankees in the vicinity of that town were the small detachment of reconnaissance cavalry which Pettigrew had observed. Pettigrew could have easily wiped them out and returned with the much-needed shoes.

Immediately Heth spoke up. Might he have permission to lead his own division over to that shoe store and relieve the proprietor of his stock?

General Hill readily granted permission, and the next morning, July 1, General Heth was on his way.

It was a complete accident, you see. No one, neither the Rebs nor the Yanks, either anticipated or intended the carnage that followed. The Confederates, so preoccupied with the advertisement in that small-town newspaper, had utterly miscalculated the size and tenacity of the Union cavalry, as well as the proximity of the First Corps and the Eleventh Corps.

So began the footwear war, a spontaneous three-day holocaust. And all the Confederates wanted were shoes from the R. F. McIlheny store.

In Gettysburg.

19. The Scarecrow

BLANCHE JANSON, seventy-two, was homeless except for the refuge of a farmhouse near the German village of Zeegendorf.

That was February of 1945, the beginning of the end for Germany in the Second World War.

And the Russians were coming. The Russians were swarming through the German countryside, looting homes, brutalizing villagers and farm families.

Yet the farmhouse where the widow Janson had sought refuge was spared the rampaging victors. For what awaited any Russian soldiers who might happen to pass by was what you might call a scarecrow. A scarecrow sewn together by Blanche Janson.

Mrs. Janson and her physician husband were American citizens living in the German city of Dresden. Dr. Janson died during the war. Blanche was elderly and alone when Dresden burst into flames.

Not even the Nazis, the masters of the inconceivable, could conceive of an Allied air attack on that glorious city. Defenseless and tactically irrelevant, Dresden had been known for centuries as a world capital of elegance, a showplace of priceless art treasures and splendid architecture, not to mention the birthplace of some of the world's finest and most famous china.

Then, in February of 1945, the unimaginable occurred. The Allies descended from the skies, and Dresden died—a death at once incredibly swift and agonizingly slow.

Twelve hundred British and American bombers, fourteen hours, sixteen hundred acres engulfed in a fiery hurricane.

Seventy-five thousand homes were destroyed. An estimated 135,000 lives were lost, twice as many as died at Hiroshima! Many were not lucky enough to die.

In the streets the mutilated living cried out, begging their fleeing neighbors to shoot them. Rescue vehicles, bound for the countryside, refused to accept any animal, no matter how small—and so hundreds of beloved pets were put to death so that their masters might be spared.

It was on one such rescue vehicle that seventy-two-year-old Blanche Janson was transported to safety after forty-eight hours of huddling in the ruins of Dresden. The remote farmhouse to which she came was almost as vulnerable as that marvelous city had been.

But Mrs. Janson survived the war and its aftermath, eventually returned to the United States—thanks to a scarecrow.

Mrs. Janson sewed it together from the clothing of fellow refugees. One woman's flannel nightgown, another woman's apron.

And the scarecrow kept at bay the notorious, victorious Russians, who otherwise would surely have ransacked the farmhouse, perhaps worse.

In fact, that farmhouse where Mrs. Janson stayed developed such a reputation for security that soon the families from neighboring farms were beseeching Blanche to safekeep their most valued possessions.

The homemade scarecrow was spared also, was handed down to Blanche's daughter, who now prizes it above all she has.

For what the resourceful Mrs. Janson had manufactured on an old treadle sewing machine, from a despised red Nazi banner and a white flannel nightgown and a blue kitchen apron, and then displayed above the farmhouse door—was "Old Glory."

The American flag.

Now you know THE REST OF THE STORY.

20. Guess Who's Coming to Dinner

JOHN AND ISABEL had a lovely home in the suburbs, a lovely quiet life. Then one day John turned to Isabel and said, "Guess who's coming to dinner."

Isabel could not guess.

And then John told her THE REST OF THE STORY.

That very evening—September 3, 1971—John's ex-wife would be coming for a visit. A long visit. She would, in fact, be staying permanently.

Now, put yourself in Isabel's place. If anyone ever had grounds for divorce, you now do. John never was a particularly easy man to live with. Now, suddenly, he wants you to share your home with a woman to whom he was once married!

Yet while you might have been on the phone to your lawyer, Isabel listened patiently to John's explanation.

His former wife had been traveling for almost twenty years. For quite some while she had disappeared in South America. At least, no one had heard from her. Eventually she turned up in West Germany, in the city of Bonn. From there it was on to Rome, then to Milan.

Now, at last, she was returning to her former husband.

It mattered not in the least that he had remarried in the intervening years. Her place was with him.

Isabel took the news calmly. After all, John was now in his seventy-fifth year. Who knew how much longer he had to live? If seeing his ex-wife fulfilled him somehow, why should Isabel deny him the opportunity?

So Isabel welcomed John's former spouse into her household.

I cannot imagine that first evening being anything but tense. The three of them seated at the candlelit dinner table—Isabel, John, and John's ex-wife, who said absolutely nothing all night. Elderly John did much reminiscing about old times. His ex-wife failed even to smile.

How then might one explain Isabel's apparent sympathy toward this strange woman? For not only did Isabel tolerate her presence, she cared for the woman from her husband's past, even fussed over her and fixed her hair!

John's ex remained cold, indifferent, expressed not the slightest gratitude. Still she stayed with John and Isabel—stayed right in their home—was present each night at the dinner table, visitors would later remark.

And that was truly remarkable.

For John's ex-wife had been dead nineteen years.

Nineteen years earlier, she had been embalmed by a master embalmer. After almost a year's labor over her lifeless body, she was virtually perfectly preserved. The job had cost a hundred thousand dollars.

And then guess what happened.

The corpse got lost.

For nineteen years John had attempted to locate his deceased wife's body, and at last in 1971 he succeeded. She was as lovely as ever.

That is why, in a lavish villa in an exclusive suburb of Madrid, Spain, a cadaver came to dinner, the object of an exiled dictator's perverse affection.

For he, John, was Argentina's own *Juan Perón.*

His former wife—a woman whose charm not even death could diminish—you remember as *Evita.*

Only now you know THE REST OF THE STORY.

21. Bad Friday

IT'S FRIDAY!

Today those words are good news. The end of the work week, the beginning of the Saturday-Sunday fun days.

But once upon a time "It's Friday" was among the least auspicious things you could say. Friday was considered completely unlucky; not only a Friday occurring on the thirteenth of the month, but *any* Friday.

Scholars, attempting to trace the origin of this superstition, have cited a number of examples.

The European tradition of executing criminals on Friday dates back to the Middle Ages. "Hangman's day," they used to call it.

There are a number of biblical examples as well. Supposedly Adam and Eve succumbed to temptation on a Friday. Similarly, it is said, the Great Flood and the fall of the Tower of Babel and the destruction of Solomon's temple began on a Friday. While it would seem that Christ's Friday crucifixion is the most likely origin, anthropologists point up that Friday was once the day of rest for certain primitive tribes and that those who worked on that day invited the least favorable fortune.

Bad Friday superstition has had no trouble attracting believers throughout the centuries. In various parts of the world there were those who refused to plant potatoes, or go courting, or even cut their fingernails on Friday. Turn a bed on Friday, it's been said, and the night will be sleepless. Once it was thought that eggs laid on Friday were the ones that went stale.

Our ancestors warned one another never to begin anything on a Friday—not a birth, nor a marriage, nor a new profession, nor, especially, a journey. Folks used to be quite reluctant to travel on Fridays. Seamen in particular.

For hundreds of years this nonsense was tolerated, until at last it tangled with an even more formidable issue: money.

It made news at the time. Even an 1891 issue of the *Scientific American* reported what had happened.

The story involved a contemporary English shipowner frustrated by his inability to find a crew willing to set sail on a Friday. The superstition was costing him and virtually everyone else in the shipping trade a lot of business.

Then one day this shipowner conceived a way to sabotage Friday phobia. He would add one more ship to his fleet of merchant vessels. He would sign every contract concerning her construction on a Friday. He would lay her keel on a Friday. He would launch her on a Friday. He would even employ Captain James Friday for her maiden voyage, which was to begin on a Friday and terminate in the East Indies on a Friday.

Naturally the vessel was christened the *Friday*.

And after the bravest, least superstitious seamen in all of England were hand-picked for her crew, the good ship *Friday* sailed toward the horizon. In doing so she had struck a blow for reality and reason.

So Friday is now welcome in our week.

We don't fear Friday anymore, in spite of what happened a century ago.

For after the merchant vessel *Friday* left port on her maiden voyage, she was never heard from again.

And now you know THE REST OF THE STORY.

22. Oscar

HIS MUSICAL STAGE PRODUCTIONS were so popular, so successful, that his competitors paid him a million dollars to get out of town.

Indeed, there was a time when he commanded more newspaper attention in New York City than anyone, with the possible exception of the president of the United States.

Millions recognized him by his first name alone.

Oscar.

His story is THE REST OF THE STORY.

When Oscar was a little boy, his dad was determined to rear a musician. Instrumental study began when the youngster was five.

Violin and piano lessons continued through Oscar's twelfth year, when he entered a conservatory to learn harmony and counterpoint. Classes in composition and music appreciation followed.

And then, when Oscar was fifteen, something happened which was to change the course of his life.

Wintertimes he loved ice skating, and there was a pond not far from his house. One evening Oscar had thus lost track of time and arrived home late for his lessons.

His enraged disciplinarian father promptly seized a belt and began thrashing the boy. The buckle cut a gash in his forehead. The wound required stitches. Later that night, after his father was asleep, Oscar left home forever.

Pawning his violin, he received enough cash to get him to New York. He never lost the scar on his forehead, nor on his heart, yet, indirectly, the incident which had caused them both gave the world something to sing about.

Oscar was broke when he arrived in the big city. His first job was making cigars. It was tedious work, so the youngster decided to make it easier. He invented a machine to do the work for him. Patenting this and other inventions, he got rich.

At last he was free to pursue his dreams—to compose music, to write plays, to become the best musical producer in New York history.

He realized all three.

Within a few brief years, Oscar's reputation flourished. He was particularly renowned for his prolificacy. One day he was having lunch with a fellow theatrical writer who dared Oscar to compose an entire musical in forty-eight hours. Oscar bet a hundred dollars that he could and was immediately escorted to a hotel room where the miracle was to be performed. Oscar succeeded, the musical was produced, and the legend grew.

And yes, it's true that after a while Oscar posed a sufficient threat to his competitors that he was bought out, handed more than a million dollars to keep his musical productions out of New York and Philadelphia and Boston and Chicago.

By now surely you have guessed that the young musician who left home after a belt-buckle beating, the theatrical wonder who composed an entire musical in two days, was Oscar Hammerstein.

And did I mention that the competitors who paid to get him out of town comprised the Metropolitan Opera Company?

For this Oscar Hammerstein never collaborated with composer Richard Rodgers. The man you have just met was Oscar Hammerstein the *First*.

He was the *grandfather* of the godfather of Broadway.

Now you know THE REST OF THE STORY.

23. Going ... Going ... Gone!

THE WORD *auction* creates a vivid impression, a clear mental picture superimposed with clattering verbosity at great velocity.

The auction tradition crosses cultures, spans the length and breadth of human history. And always with that one humorous potential: the bidder, swept away by the excitement of the event, ultimately in possession of something he really didn't need.

That is just the way it happened one fine spring day, almost 1,800 years ago.

And you won't know whether to laugh or to cry when you learn THE REST OF THE STORY.

His name was Marcus Didius Julianus, product of a prominent family, native of the city which is now Milan, Italy.

He would have liked us to remember all the impressive things he did and the important positions he held, his distinguished service in the army, his provincial governorships.

Fact is, his principal distinction was his vast wealth.

Marcus was loaded.

It was perhaps for that reason that he loved auctions. Marcus could bid with confidence. Anything he wanted badly enough, he would almost always outbid the other bidders to get.

One day late in March 193 A.D., Marcus heard about an auction being held in the camp of some praetorian guards.

Marcus attended.

Actually, the praetorians were auctioning only one "item," an old relic that had seen better days.

At first Marcus wondered what in the world he would ever do with it.

"But what a bargain!" exclaimed the praetorian auctioneer. Since each of the guards would share equally in the profit, the price would be designated per man. The bidding began at ten thousand sesterces.

A bargain indeed! Marcus raised his hand.

Ten thousand sesterces to Marcus Julianus! Do I hear twenty thousand?

Another bidder, fellow named Flavius, raised *his* hand. Twenty thousand once . . . twice . . .

Marcus couldn't stand it. "Twenty-five thousand!" he shouted.

Sold to Marcus Julianus for twenty-five thousand sesterces!

But there's an ancient saying, isn't there? *Caveat emptor.* Let the buyer beware.

Surely that would apply to a bidder at an auction as well. And to one in particular: Marcus Didius Julianus. Two months later, his expensive toy turned on him, killed him.

He really didn't need that devaluing piece of real estate. But he just couldn't pass up the prestige accompanying the highest bid.

Interesting, how centuries past speak to the present.

In ancient Rome, the praetorian guards were sort of an agency, were supposed to defend legal authority. And they wound up usurping it. They mutinied. And they sold out to the highest bidder. Actually auctioned *the entire Roman Empire.*

So for two months, anyway, Marcus Julianus was emperor of Rome.

This is history.

The once glorious late-great nation-state went not with a bang, but quietly going . . . going . . . gone . . . forever.

That is THE REST OF THE STORY.

24. Little Jackie Took an Ax

IN SO MANY WAYS, Mrs. Joy reflected her name.

She was especially kind, sympathetic, a good listener, and, when sought as such, a wise adviser.

It was perhaps for all those reasons that Mrs. Joy's neighbor came calling that day.

The woman had a problem. She had to confide in someone. The problem was her son, fifteen-year-old Jack.

"Was Jack ill?" inquired Mrs. Joy.

The neighbor lady nodded. There was something terribly wrong with young Jack.

The boy had never ever been entirely physically well. He had always been plagued by a variety of maladies. Boils, bad back, flat feet, poor eyesight.

Lately Jack had been getting into trouble at school. More trouble than usual. He had been starting fights, even though he was too frail and skinny to do anything but take a beating.

Jack had also been complaining of headaches. Blinding, awful headaches. They were getting worse. Sometimes the pain was so unbearable that Jack would bang his head against the wall. Then, realizing he could not drive the pain out, he would become violent. Uncontrollably so.

The neighbor woman was quiet for a moment, biting her lip, fighting back the tears. Then she continued.

Jack was becoming suicidal, she said. He wanted to kill himself. And she, his mother, was certain he would one day succeed. Unless he killed someone else first.

That was the real trouble with Jack.

The other day he had attacked his older brother Norman. His brother, six years his senior. Jack had threatened him and then actually chased him—with an ax!

What now, the distraught mother asked, could she possibly do?

Mrs. Joy was a compassionate, well-intentioned woman, although I'm not certain why she offered the particular advice which ultimately she did.

Surely she was trying to be helpful, if perhaps she was groping at straws, when she suggested young Jack be taken to see a nutritionist—a self-professed physical-fitness expert who was scheduled to speak before the Oakland Women's Club.

Remember, this was a half-century ago, before there was such a thing as a nationwide "health fad."

And yet Jack's mother took the boy to that lecture.

The speaker was an energetic gentleman in his fifties named Paul Bragg. His doctrine was simple and straightforward: natural foods, regular exercise. But he electrified his listeners with his boundless enthusiasm. And finally, to dramatize the rewards of the way of life he espoused, Mr. Bragg did handsprings across the stage.

After the lecture, long after the rest of the audience had gone home, one spellbound boy remained to talk privately with the inspiring gentleman.

And that night young Jack was reborn.

Following the prescriptions of Paul Bragg, Jack thereafter voluntarily omitted meat and refined sugar from his diet. He even started exercising.

Jack, who until his fifteenth year was plagued by boils and bad back and flat feet and poor eyesight and chronic fatigue, the frail youngster whose blinding headaches made him want to die and whose violent temper born of constant agony once compelled him to chase his brother with an ax, that same young man was destined to lead a completely happy, totally healthy life.

At sixty-five years of age, he could do 1,033 pushups in 23 minutes, could swim a mile while towing 13 rowboats filled with 76 people!

He was a sick old man at fifteen.

He would be young ever after.

And his name became synonymous with physical fitness: *Jack LaLanne.*

That is THE REST OF THE STORY.

25. The Old Clock in the George Hotel

ONCE UPON A TIME, in Piercebridge, North Yorkshire, England, there was a charming traveler's haven known as the George Hotel. It may be there still.

More than a hundred years ago, the hotel was a routine stop for horse-drawn coaches. The place was run by two bachelor brothers named Jenkins.

There was an old clock in the lobby of the George Hotel, and that is really what this story is about. The old clock.

It kept very good time. Such excellent time that its accuracy was a frequent topic of conversation among hotel guests.

Then one of the Jenkins brothers died. Strangely, suddenly, the old clock began losing time. Five, ten minutes a day at first. Eventually a half-hour, forty-five minutes, sometimes as much as an hour a day!

The most skilled clockmakers did their best to repair the ailing timepiece. Each failed. The clock's chronic unreliability became as remarkable as its precision had once been.

Since the clock had started getting crotchety shortly after the death of the younger Jenkins brother, some said it was no wonder that when the elder brother passed away in his ninetieth year the old clock in the lobby of the George Hotel, fully wound, nevertheless stopped completely!

The new hotel manager never attempted to have the clock repaired. He just left it sitting silently in a sunlit corner, its hands resting in the position they had assumed the moment old man Jenkins died.

During the mid-1870s, an American songwriter named

Henry Clay Work traveled to England. Visiting Piercebridge, he was told the story of the old clock in the George Hotel. Seeing the clock for himself, Henry was inspired to compose a song about it—about the fascinating coincidence of its stopping as its elderly owner breathed his last.

Henry Work was a Connecticut-born printer's apprentice who studied harmony so he could write songs for his friends. In 1861, his songs started selling. You may remember his rousing Civil War anthem *Marching Through Georgia*. During his trip to England, that was Henry's most popular tune.

But now Henry Work wanted to eclipse his *Marching Through Georgia* success, and he decided to do it with a song about a clock that stopped ticking when its aged owner died.

Henry wrote that song. And it became the success of his lifetime, selling almost a million copies of sheet music.

One of the things that made it so appealing was the way the lyrics were written. Henry pretended he was old man Jenkins' grandchild, recalling the clock which ran for ninety years and then stopped forever.

Although you may never have heard that song, you are familiar with a derivative phrase.

For prior to the lyrics of Henry Work, such tall-standing, long-case clocks were called "pendulum" or "pandalome" or "coffin" clocks.

It was Henry Work who wrote:

> *My grandfather's clock was too tall for the shelf*
> *So it stood ninety years on the floor.*
> *It was taller by half than the old man himself*
> *Though it weighed not a pennyweight more.*

Before that song was written, long-case clocks were referred to by a variety of names. But because of Henry's verse, we have ever since called them "grandfather clocks."

Now you know THE REST OF THE STORY.

26. Five Minutes to Live

FYODOR MIKHAILOVICH was awakened at 4:00 A.M. and hustled off to jail. He was not told why. He would not have to ask. Fyodor had been spouting socialism, had been reading forbidden literature,. had been keeping company with enemies of the czar.

Fyodor's subversive friends were also rounded up that morning. They all spent months in jail before being tried for conspiracy. They were never informed of a verdict. In fact, it was not until the predawn darkness of December 22 that Fyodor and fourteen comrades were taken from their cells and transported to a nearby parade ground. A large crowd—thousands—waited silently in the biting cold and freshly fallen snow.

There was a railed platform draped in black and guarded by soldiers. Fyodor and the other prisoners were ordered to stand there.

A court clerk stepped forward. Each man was declared guilty of crimes against the czar—and condemned to die.

At first Fyodor refused to believe it. Then a comrade named Durov pointed to a cart bearing their coffins.

A priest read from the scripture, preached briefly on "the wages of sin." His voice trembled. When the priest had finished, the condemned men were made to remove their outer clothing and to put on hooded white linen shirts. These would be their shrouds.

The first three prisoners were led from the scaffold to separate posts where each was bound. A firing squad was poised fifteen paces away. Fyodor was next in line. He would be next to die.

What strange thoughts raced through Fyodor's head during those agonizing moments . . .

If only he had been condemned to live high up on some rock, on a ledge so narrow that there was only room to stand! Far better to remain standing there for all eternity, surrounded by nothingness, than to face death! Only to live, no matter how!

Desperately Fyodor tried to calculate the time left to him. Five minutes, surely that was all. His heart pounded as though it would burst. Five minutes of life! How would he spend those precious five minutes? Two he would spend saying good-bye to his comrades. Two would be reserved for his last thoughts. And in his final minute he would simply look around him, just gaze at the wonderful world he was leaving behind.

How was it possible, Fyodor demanded in silence, that now he lived and minutes later he would not? Not far away a cathedral cupola gleamed in the sunlight. Perhaps those rays of light were the elements of his transfiguration. Perhaps he would merge with them somehow at the moment of his death.

Suddenly Fyodor was calm. He was not sorry to die. He wished only that it were done.

The firing squad was given its command: "Ready . . . aim . . ."

And that is when a government messenger arrived with a document in his hand. The czar had commuted the sentences of the subversives from death to various terms of hard labor.

Fyodor was to spend four years in Siberia, four more of mandatory service in the army. But I wonder when they told him THE REST OF THE STORY.

The czar had never intended to have the subversives shot. The preparations for execution and the last-minute reprieve had been staged to demonstrate the czar's mercy and to teach the radical socialists a lesson—December 22, 1849.

And should you read the magnificent Russian novels, *Crime and Punishment* and *The Idiot*, then to be awed by the world's most vivid descriptions of a condemned man's thoughts, you'll remember the young author who survived a firing squad and Siberia, the man who had five minutes to live and lived to tell—Fyodor Mikhailovich Dostoevski.

27. The Minister Who Fought Abolition

THE AMERICAN REVOLUTION was two years under way and John Chavis, a boy of fifteen, was enlisting in the Continental Army. I mention John's service in our war for independence because in later years he would speak of it often and with much pride. It would please him that he is remembered as a patriot.

After the shooting had stopped and the states were united, John attended Princeton University, then named Washington Academy.

Shortly after the turn of the century, he passed from the role of educated to that of educator. Over the next twenty-three years, he would operate schools in four North Carolina counties. Some of his students subsequently became governors, congressmen, diplomats, each doubtless greatly influenced by John's sociopolitical philosophy.

John was an avid *anti*-abolitionist.

In an era of arguments on both sides, he wanted the slaves to stay slaves.

John held this position not only as a slave owner, which he was, but as a social theorist who claimed knowledge of what was best for his country.

The Africans were lucky to be here under *any* circumstances, he declared. He expressed a fear of slave uprisings which might result from abolitionist encouragement. "Abominable wretches," he called the abolitionists. "I would advise Americans to be on the alert for these abominable wretches."

In any event, he contended, freedom would be infinitely harder on the slaves than slavery.

John was not merely an opinionated Revolutionary War veteran, not just another self-serving slave owner, not only a reactionary educator interested in preserving the established social order. John was a Presbyterian minister!

Now, let me sketch you a little Presbyterian profile, vintage 1800. The church felt a keen sense of responsibility toward black people. Church authorities deplored slavery, considered it a national evil, were eager for the religious and secular education of blacks.

Yet there was John, a Presbyterian minister, proclaiming the nation's greatest enemy to be the abolitionist!

Slaves, John insisted, were personal property, period. It was the slave owner's right to do with the slave as he pleased.

John said: "The laws of the land declare that no legislative body shall pass a law to take away the property of a man without making remuneration. And here I would ask, has Congress the means at hand to remunerate the slave owners?"

John was deeply concerned that slavery might end suddenly one day. Even more deeply concerned over the tactics of the abolitionists.

Because John was both a renowned educator and a widely respected minister, because so many of his flock and friends and former pupils were in positions of influence, John's impact on the national conscience was considerable.

John Chavis preached to white men and women from his pulpit and taught white children in his classrooms the dangers of abolition and the right of free men to own slaves. And this doctrine which he believed with all his heart was particularly impressive coming from John Chavis, a Revolutionary War veteran, a learned theologian, a slave owner, a free man, a *black* man!

That is THE REST OF THE STORY.

28. The Suez Lighthouse

In 1856, Frenchman Auguste Bartholdi vacationed in Egypt.

Despite the strange food, the ubiquitous flies, the oppressive heat, and the continual disorder which might be referred to as Pharoah's Revenge, the young man was entirely captivated by that exotic and wonder-filled land.

Auguste especially admired the Egyptian art and architecture. The marvelous ancient sculptures. The sheer surfaces and the clear, forceful lines.

Bigness had always awed Auguste. And now here he was, his feet in the sands where bigness was born. The Pyramids. The Sphinx. The Nile. How incredible, the Frenchman mused, that a solitary pathway for the transportation of pyramid stones would take a hundred thousand men ten years to make!

Seeing the myriad man-made marvels for himself, Auguste was driven to an inexorable conclusion: All true art expresses the power of an idea. Remember that as you learn THE REST OF THE STORY.

For during the young man's Egyptian adventure he met and befriended a fellow Frenchman named Ferdinand de Lesseps. And Ferdinand had an appropriately grand-scale dream for this grand-scale land.

He wanted to join the Mediterranean and the Red Sea by a watery thread, a passageway for ships, linking East to West, across the great Isthmus of Suez.

Such an accomplishment would reduce a voyage of thousands of miles around the African continent to one of 105.

Ferdinand's plan was considered mildly amusing by most.

Young Auguste not only took it seriously, he suggested a contribution of his own.

When Ferdinand had finished his waterway, he, Auguste, would build a lighthouse at its entrance. A huge lighthouse, twice the size of the Sphinx. More than a mere structure, it would express an idea: the beacon of Western civilization shining eastward.

Ferdinand was intrigued by Auguste's proposal, and both men agreed that their dreams deserved to come true.

Ferdinand's did.

In 1859, having won the approval of the authorities concerned, Ferdinand began the challenging project which would require a decade to complete. And today the whole world takes for granted—the Suez Canal.

As for Auguste, he spent years refining a design for the Suez lighthouse. While the canal was under construction he made sketches and clay models, each varying slightly from the others, until at last he was satisfied.

Yet, while he encountered much enthusiasm for his creation, even among members of the Egyptian government, the Frenchman did not discover what his lighthouse needed most: the money to build it.

You would have liked his design. Quite original.

It was a lighthouse in the shape of a colossal, robed woman, one arm stretched heavenward, a torch in her hand.

Its rejection was not a total loss, however.

I understand that a few years later, another country sought the services of sculptor Auguste Bartholdi and received them.

All your life you have been under the impression that the Statue of Liberty was designed especially, exclusively for us.

Well—now you know THE REST OF THE STORY.

29. The Last Stagecoach Robbery

THE STAGECOACH CLATTERED through the wilderness over a trail too dusty for weak lungs, too rolling and rugged for weak stomachs. It was the stage out of Riverside bound for Globe, Arizona, mid-journey, somewhere in Kane Springs Canyon. There was a driver and a shotgun rider aboard. One passenger was a Chinese gentleman, another the treasurer of Pinal County.

Suddenly two horsemen thundered out of nowhere. Bandits, bold in that neither was masked.

Guns drawn, the outlaws halted the stage. "Do what I tell you and nobody gets hurt!" The gruff voice of the leader. No question as to which of the bandits was in charge. The other, later identified as Joe Boot, was meekly taking orders.

The Chinese passenger parted with over a hundred dollars, the Pinal County treasurer even more.

All in all, the outlaws' haul was $431. Firing menacing shots skyward, the robbers galloped off, leaving their victims with trembling hands in the air.

Minutes passed, until at last all was quiet in Kane Springs Canyon on the Arizona stagecoach trail.

Only historians would retrospectively appreciate THE REST OF THE STORY.

For this stagecoach robbery, which took place during the summer of 1898, was the last recorded stagecoach holdup in the history of the American West. A sensational event at the time.

Second-banana badman Joe Boot gave the authorities no

trouble. When the two outlaws were apprehended days later in the San Pedro Valley, both were taken to the county jail. Joe Boot stayed put. His bolder boss made a break for it, clawed through a jailhouse wall and fled into New Mexico.

Within several days more, the bandit leader Hart was re-captured at Deming.

Hart's trial was rather spectacular. During the proceedings, two little old ladies reportedly approached the thief, requesting an autograph for their little niece back home. Hart granted the request.

November 18, the last of the stagecoach bandits was sentenced to five years in the penitentiary at Yuma.

Hart proved even meaner behind bars than running free. Opium deprivation at first, eventually just plain meanness for the sake of it.

The former outlaw was paroled in 1902, on the condition that Hart depart Arizona permanently.

This same one-time stagecoach bandit opened a cigar and tobacco shop in Kansas City and was arrested once more in 1904, this time for fencing stolen goods.

The history books sometimes refer to Hart as a "low creature," glint-in-the-eye hardened, foul-mouthed, illiterate—however, absolutely stunning in a dress!

For the last of the Wild West stagecoach bandits, the outlaw no badman dared cross, was no man—was *Pearl* Hart, a holdup woman!

30. Flynn's Foil

LATE-SHOW DEVOTEES will recall a rip-roaring melodrama, vintage 1942, entitled *Desperate Journey.*

Some big names in the cast: Raymond Massey, Alan Hale, Arthur Kennedy, Ronald Sinclair, and of course the star, dashing Errol Flynn.

The movie is about a British Royal Air Force flight crew, shot down and imprisoned by the Nazis. The good guys escape, making their way slowly, arduously across Germany toward Holland and the coast. The Nazis launch a massive manhunt. Meanwhile, the men they are hunting procure Nazi uniforms. Somehow they must get out of the country undetected, for as POWs they have obtained information of inestimable value to the Allies.

Errol Flynn, who played Lieutenant Forbes in *Desperate Journey,* had a real-life raucous, irascible reputation. Scandal followed him like a hungry hyena. His life ricocheted back and forth between beauty and the bottle. Flynn was also fond of terrorizing his associates. He once decked director John Huston in a public brawl. Another time he stuffed a live snake into Olivia de Havilland's underwear.

There was one colleague upon whom Flynn particularly enjoyed heaping lighthearted abuse. That colleague costarred with Errol in *Santa Fe Trail.* One scene in that movie required a number of men to leap on their horses and gallop away. It was the saddle of the aforementioned costar which Flynn surreptitiously loosened before shooting began. Predictably, the prank left Flynn's fellow actor dazed in the dust.

It was this same fellow actor who costarred with Errol Flynn in *Desperate Journey*. And that brings us to another backstage scene which must be set. . . .

When Warner Brothers informed Flynn that the *Desperate Journey* shooting schedule would intrude on Saturdays, the temperamental leading man became even more so. Furious is what he was. So he plotted his revenge against the studio.

One Saturday morning, before the actors were due on the set, Errol invited the entire cast into his dressing room. Even in those spacious quarters there was barely enough room, but there was more than enough Bourbon.

His plan was to sabotage the Saturday shooting by getting everyone drunk. He failed, however, to notice that his costar was emptying each papercup refill of the hard stuff into a nearby spittoon.

On the set at 11:00 A.M., the first scene of the day's shooting was to open with a line spoken by that actor.

And he, completely sober, delivered it perfectly.

Flynn, his eyes refusing to focus, gazed in the direction of his colleague for a long, incredulous moment. Then suddenly, in a burst of inebriate outrage, Flynn flung a staggering epithet. His goat had been got. The rascal had been repaid for a prank as never before.

And Flynn's foil, the young actor who kept his head when all about him were seeing double, the costar irascible Errol could not fool twice, was Ronald Reagan.

Now you know THE REST OF THE STORY.

31. The All-American House

WOULD ANDREW JACKSON or William Henry Harrison or Abraham Lincoln ever have been elected to the U.S. presidency without evoking the popular campaign symbol of the log cabin?

Bill Harrison, for instance, was born on his family's fabulous Virginia plantation. His daddy was a wealthy and politically prominent man. But the image that appealed to the voters who voted for him was summed up in the slogan: "Log cabin and hard cider."

The log cabin is the all-American house.

To the schoolchild it still represents our grass roots origins, our pioneer virtues. Its appearance was as rugged and its resistance to the elements as hardy as the American spirit itself. Perhaps most significant of all, a properly constructed log cabin would last for many generations. A dwelling of humble origin, yet as enduring as the American Dream.

Usually only two metal tools were required to build a log cabin: an ax, of course, to fell the trees and hew the logs; and a wedge-shaped cleaving tool called a froe, which was needed to rive shingles or roof boards.

Often a frontier cabin contained not one piece of iron, no iron hinges nor even a single iron nail. Sometimes the pioneers built temporary log cabins in which even the chimneys were made of logs and clay. Sometimes the crevices between the logs were filled with moss. This was merely to insulate. The logs themselves were securely attached by corner notches.

At Thanksgiving time, myriad mental pictures arise from the Pilgrim heritage we learned in school: wild turkeys and Indian corn and black hats with buckles and bell-muzzled blunderbuss muskets and hazy harvest moons—and cozy log cabins.

After exploring the North American coastline for more than a month, our Pilgrim forefathers parked the *Mayflower* in Plymouth Bay and went searching for a site for their settlement. It was Christmas Day, 1620.

The Pilgrims' first "permanent" dwelling and utility house was constructed immediately. It was twenty feet square. Two weeks later it burned, and the resident Pilgrim shore party scurried back to the *Mayflower*, where they spent the remainder of the winter.

At the first sign of spring they were ashore again, tilling fields and building cabins. Fortunately the Pilgrims had brought with them a wide variety of tools: broad axes, pitching axes, chisels, augers, whipsaws, two-handed saws, froes, and so on. They had nails of every sort. And before the *Mayflower* returned to England that April, seven small cabins were standing.

It was Governor William Bradford who called them "cabins."

But they were not log cabins, nor was the larger structure they had erected before New Year's.

Nor were the buildings of Jamestown colony in Virginia, a dozen years before.

Nor were the shelters of the Puritan colonists, who would not arrive for almost a decade.

The men we now recognize as our founding fathers, from Jamestown on, built everything from frame houses to thatched huts to tents.

But no log cabins!

Two centuries later this young nation would glorify the log cabin as the all-American house, the symbol of our earliest heritage. Yet the first one appeared on the North American landscape in 1638, in a colony in the lower Delaware Valley.

Those colonists built log cabins because *their* forefathers had built them. *Thousands* of years before.

They were not Jamestown Virginians, nor Pilgrims, nor Puritans.

They, who eventually taught the English to build log cabins, were *Swedish*.

Now you know THE REST OF THE STORY.

32. Sweet Kiss

In 1923 Frank Hayes was thirty-five, resident of Brooklyn, New York.

Frank was a horse trainer. He trained horses for straightaway races and steeplechases.

You know what a steeplechase is, sort of an equestrian obstacle course with hedges and walls and water-filled ditches.

At any rate, Frank Hayes trained horses to run those courses.

He was not a professional jockey, much as he longed to be. He had ridden in one race, failing then even to place. That was the extent of his actual racing experience.

Still Frank's unrealistic dream kept nagging him, his dream of riding a horse to victory in a real race—just once! He was a horse trainer who had always wanted to be a jockey.

His equestrian colleagues advised that Frank should stick with what he knew best: training. Anyway, at thirty-five he was just too old to be competing with the youngsters who were then winning the big purses.

Frank understood the age factor. He understood that if he were ever to ride in and win a race, it would have to be soon.

He begged his horse-owner employer for an opportunity. That opportunity was granted.

Frank would ride in the June 4 Belmont Park steeplechase.

That would be Frank's second race ever, was to be his last chance to win. This was also true of the horse he was scheduled to ride, a gallant but aged bay mare named Sweet Kiss. Perhaps one good steeplechase race left in her, one last opportunity to distinguish her own theretofore undistinguished career.

The afternoon of June 4 they were poised at the post, two has-beens who never were, Frank Hayes and his mount, Sweet Kiss. A two-mile course of twelve jumps lay before them.

It would be difficult to imagine who was more surprised, the spectators or jockey Frank Hayes himself. At the mile, Frank and Sweet Kiss, twenty-to-one underdogs, were still leading the pack, were in fact two lengths ahead of the horse most favored to win.

It was at the beginning of the second mile that the odds-on favorite charged forward. Now the younger horse and his younger jockey were neck and neck with Sweet Kiss and rider Frank.

They stayed almost even, the young "team" gaining slightly on the straight and level, and the elder gaining slightly in the jumps.

In the last turn, heading into the homestretch, Sweet Kiss swerved, almost collided with another horse. For a fleeting second it seemed an error from which the old mare could not possibly recover.

But she did recover. She did straighten out in the stretch. And by a length and a half, *Sweet Kiss did win.*

Surely it had been one of the most exciting steeplechases ever run at Belmont Park.

What a sweet victory for Sweet Kiss and her jockey Frank Hayes, the twenty-to-one underdogs some believed "too old" to race!

At least I hope Frank somehow knew that his dream had been realized, that he had gone the distance and won.

For, according to eyewitnesses, it appeared to have happened in the last turn, before the last jump, when Sweet Kiss swerved momentarily off course. In all probability, that is when Frank's heart slipped out from under him.

You see, his head never lifted from the old mare's neck, not even after they crossed the finish line together.

As never before nor since in horseracing history, a race had been won by an over-the-hill horse—and a dead man.

Now you know THE REST OF THE STORY.

33. Francis

WHERE HAVE THE HYSTERICAL teenage audiences gone? In the 1960s frantic, grimacing young girls swooned over the Beatles. In the fifties their older sisters went wild at the sight or sound of Elvis Presley.

In the forties it was someone else.

His name was Francis, although I don't believe anybody ever called him that.

Now we are going to call him that.

What Francis did to the young women of his generation—their pysches, their souls—was positively astounding. How quickly we forget.

During performances they leaped from their seats and rushed toward the stage. They threw bouquets of flowers and jewelry and sometimes articles of clothing. They wept. They screamed. They fainted. They behaved in every bizarre manner imaginable.

A stodgy old physician was once asked to describe, in his own terms, the effect of Francis on the feminine listeners. He attended a personal appearance and came away shaking his head, speaking of magnetism and electricity and contagion, of histrionic epilepsy and sexual arousal and even of a phenomenon which had seemed identical to that of tickling!

Indeed, no one ever before in the history of show business had held his fans under such a spell.

Teenagers and older women clawed and scratched and fought like roller-derby amazons over souvenirs. Anything would do, as long as he had touched it. Young ladies often dashed toward him with scissors, hoping to abscond with a lock of hair. One woman actually seized the butt of a cigar she had watched Francis smoke, then carried it in her bosom for years, some say forever after.

And there were groupies in the forties, if we may call them that. The ones who waited for Francis at his hotel. The ones who followed him from town to town on tour, some even disguising themselves as men so they could get unobtrusively closer to him.

The profound devotion of his admirers made Francis perhaps the wealthiest performer of his day. And he spent money lavishly. At one time he had no fewer than 60 expensively tailored jackets and 365 ties.

Manufacturers capitalized on his celebrity, flooding their various markets for more than a decade with clothing and jewelry and even candy merchandised under Francis' name.

His egomania was staggering. A superstar, he never let anyone forget it. He thrived on adulation and could not bear to lose the spotlight, on- or offstage. In fact, a great conflict existed between his innate love of solitude and his need for a fawning entourage.

Bad press, and there was much of it, often drove him into a profane fist-shaking frenzy. Yet it should be noted that Francis vigorously encouraged the gossip regarding his sporadic misbehavior, his sometimes impertinence in the presence of VIPs.

Also there were fine qualities, kindness and generosity, which offset his constant pride and occasional irascibility.

Music aside, however, the world of entertainment will longest remember Francis' sex appeal. Even as a much older man, he never failed to attract women.

So perhaps it was envy, in part, that inspired so many of his colleagues to minimize the accomplishments of the dazzling performer with the shoulder-length hair and the outrageous tight-fitting costumes.

He was the first one-man show in the history of the concert stage, the mesmerizing pianist-composer of the *1840s* who turned a generation upside down.

Francis, in Hungarian, "Ferencz."

He called himself Franz.

Franz Liszt.

Now you know THE REST OF THE STORY.

34. The Batter and the Blonde

IT WAS TO BE the grandest, most exciting wedding the city of San Francisco had ever seen. The fairy tale marriage of the batter and the blonde.

The month was November. Baseball season was over. The groom had been named his team's most valuable player, also major league player of the year. He had been courting the beautiful Hollywood actress for more than two years. In the early stages of their romance the handsome outfielder had denied they were more than acquaintances. The denial quickly lost its credibility. And now the world-famous couple was about to be wed in the most joyous, enthusiastic atmosphere imaginable.

To San Franciscans, especially to the North Beach area's population of Italian-Americans, the baseball player was very much the local hero and more, a living legend. Anyone he chose to marry would have been all right with those admirers. Yet his bride was not just anyone. She was a screen goddess, captor of the nation's imagination.

The ceremony at the Cathedral of Saints Peter and Paul was intriguing to everyone, sports fans and moviegoers alike. A crowd had already begun to gather in the predawn darkness. By sunup the streets near the church were virtually impassable, even though the wedding had not been scheduled to take place until two in the afternoon. There were traffic jams for miles around all morning long.

As the hour of the ceremony drew near, there were thousands outside the cathedral. In the suffocating throng a woman collapsed. Police, who had lost control of the crowd long before, now had to use their nightsticks to clear a path to the ambulance.

It took the wedding party more than a half-hour to battle its way through the mob. Well-wishers went wild when they caught sight of the baseball-hero groom. It was a quarter past two before the bridesmaids could make it to the church door. The radiant Hollywood-actress bride was delayed even longer by devotees.

The groom's brother, accidentally locked outside at the front door, struggled to a side door. That door opened for him, but he was almost trampled by gate-crashers.

One guest flashed his invitation and promptly muscled in a half-dozen members of his own family who had not been authorized to attend. Forged invitations were a continual nuisance. One man presenting such a counterfeit later confessed that he had paid a hundred dollars for it.

The standing-room-only crowd inside witnessed a charming service. Formal, of course. The bride's white satin Grecian-style gown was dazzling.

The couple seemed so happy. Yet the fairy tale of the batter and the blonde was also a reality, and so, as it sometimes happens, they did not live happily ever after. The magical marriage which had begun as the largest public wedding in the history of San Francisco ended less than five years later in divorce.

By now surely you have guessed that the handsome baseball superstar whose wedding attracted more attention than his major-league statistics was the "Yankee Clipper," the one and only "Joltin' Joe" DiMaggio.

I did want you to meet his bride, though. An enchanting, young, blond Hollywood actress named Dorothy Arnold.

Dorothy Arnold's 1939 marriage to Joe DiMaggio was eventually forgotten by most of us. The reason is Joe's second marriage, to another enchanting young lady—named Marilyn Monroe.

Now you know THE REST OF THE STORY.

35. The Perfect Helmet

ONE MORE HARD HIT might have been the end of Roger Staubach—so he quit. The incomparable Dallas Cowboys quarterback, plagued by concussions a couple of seasons ago, decided enough was enough and left the NFL.

Suddenly the fans who had once been so preoccupied with Namath's knees were now discussing head injuries as though they were something new to football.

Most seasons, head injuries rank fifth, comprising approximately one in twenty of all pro football injuries. The head is vulnerable in other sports as well. Ask the baseball player who has just been beaned by a ninety-seven-mile-an-hour fastball, or the retired boxer with the cauliflower brain.

There may be no hope for the pugilist, whose sport is based directly on the receipt and avoidance of physical punishment above the belt. Nor perhaps for the race car driver who rams an embankment doing a hundred and fifty. But for the less drastic crashes, for the motorcyclist who tags car nineteen in the twenty-car jump, for the batter who gets decked and the quarterback who gets sacked, the life-or-death difference may rest with the protective headgear the sportsman is wearing. That is why this next is important.

Four American researchers, writing in the respected British medical journal, the *Lancet*, believe they have discovered the design for the perfect helmet, an equipment design that might have kept Roger Staubach with the Cowboys for another decade.

The design objective of the modern football helmet is to

disperse a specific impact over as large a surface area as possible. In a good football helmet that area of dispersement should be approximately twenty square inches, with the minimum of the impact being transferred to the skull. To achieve this level of effectiveness, a helmet must be perfectly fitted to the wearer. The most common of the football helmets currently in use is the suspension type, which has an inner canvas web, sponge-rubber padding, and an outer plastic shell. But the reason serious head injuries can and do occur, even when this particular football helmet is worn, is best understood when one considers the physical shock a football player is often expected to endure.

It takes an impact of about 425 pounds per square inch to fracture the human skull. Football players—high school, college, pro—sometimes get hit in the head with a force of 300 *Gs*, or 300 times their own body weight! The duration of the impact is also a factor, but the figures remain.

Therefore, these four researchers set out to design the ultimately protective sports helmet. At the conclusion of their study, this was the essence of their recommendation to equipment manufacturers: a helmet which would be "lighter, thicker, form-fitting, firm but spongy . . . with a relatively thin and hard outer shell to protect against abrasion. Wherever practical, this should be combined with a protective neck collar to dampen sudden, unexpected rotatory movements that could create shearing strains in brain tissue."

Now it can be told. The four researchers who advanced that design in the *Lancet*—borrowed it. The perfect crash helmet had already been in use for thousands of years, but it was only recently that scientists realized why it worked so well.

The ultimate impact-absorbing helmet, an athletic-equipment manufacturer's dream, is *the skull of the woodpecker*.

Now you know THE REST OF THE STORY.

36. Annie Walked Out

ANNIE WAS EMPLOYED by the nation's largest clothing manufacturer, Hart, Schaffner & Marx. When the company announced a salary cut for its employees, Annie walked out—just walked off the job. Annie Shapiro took sixteen other garment workers with her. And so began one of the toughest strikes in Chicago history.

On September 22, the seventeen garment workers stormed out of the contract shop at Eighteenth and Halsted streets. That was Hart, Schaffner & Marx shop number five. As contract shops went, it was not a bad working environment. The walkout was clearly the result of a recent cut in pay.

It would take three weeks for the walkout to become a full-fledged strike of Hart, Schaffner & Marx employees. There were more than two thousand strikers, and by the middle of October they were threatening the workers who had remained on the job. Hart, Schaffner & Marx actually had to hire bodyguards to protect their loyal employees from striker violence.

And the strike spread.

Workers from Kuppenheimer and Hirsch-Wickwire and other clothing firms were beginning to strike in sympathy. It was not until November, however, that the strikers began seeking the aid of established organizations.

A delegation of garment workers approached the Women's Trade Union League. Another group of strikers appealed to the Chicago Federation of Labor. Meanwhile,

Annie—remember Annie Shapiro, the young lady whose spontaneous walkout had inspired the whole thing?—Annie was making speeches to social organizations and reporters. She would walk even into bars and start preaching her cause.

Violence continued to mount. Early in December, a striker was shot and killed while harassing a scab. The bodyguard who did the shooting was almost killed himself by an angry mob. Thirty thousand sympathizers attended the fallen striker's funeral.

A few days later there was a skirmish between strikers and strikebreakers. In the free-for-all another striker was killed, this time by a policeman.

And more violence.

Shortly before Christmas, an eighteen-year-old boy was making a delivery for a nonunion tailor shop. Three men ambushed him, shot him to death. His mother said he had been threatened before and had intended to quit his job the next day.

Within days, more killings, including that of a guard for Hart, Schaffner & Marx.

Then on February 3, four and a half months after the strike had begun, the president of the United Garment Workers called off the strike. The employees of Chicago clothing manufacturers returned to their jobs in defeat.

As for the salary cut at Hart, Schaffner & Marx's shop number five, the reduction in pay which had inspired Annie Shapiro and her friends to walk out in the first place, that salary cut stood. Annie and her fellow workers returned to work under virtually the same conditions they had fled.

Students of social history maintain that the garment workers' strike of 1910 led, at least indirectly, to the establishment of the Amalgamated Clothing Workers of America. Mostly forgotten is this:

Annie Shapiro had been sewing pockets in men's pants for

four cents apiece. Her employer reduced that wage rate to three and three-quarters cents.

That means Annie walked out, and tens of thousands struck in sympathy, and a half-dozen people were killed—over one-fourth of one penny.

Now you know THE REST OF THE STORY.

37. Sparky Was a Loser

WHEN HE WAS a little boy the other children called him "Sparky," after a comic-strip horse named Sparkplug. Sparky never did shake that nickname.

School was all but impossible for Sparky. He failed every subject in the eighth grade. Every subject! He flunked physics in high school. Receiving a flat zero in the course, he distinguished himself as the worst physics student in his school's history.

He also flunked Latin. And algebra. And English.

He didn't do much better in sports. Although he managed to make the school golf team, he promptly lost the only important match of the year.

There was a consolation match. Sparky lost that too.

Throughout his youth Sparky was awkward socially. He was not actually disliked by the other youngsters. No one cared that much. He was astonished if a classmate ever said hello to him outside school hours. No way to tell how he might have done at dating. In high school Sparky never once asked a girl out. He was too afraid of being turned down.

Sparky was a loser. He, his classmates, everyone knew it. So he rolled with it. Sparky made up his mind early in life that if things were meant to work out, they would. Otherwise, he would content himself with what appeared to be inevitable mediocrity.

But this is THE REST OF THE STORY.

One something was important to Sparky: drawing. He was proud of his own artwork. Of course, no one else appreciated

it. In his senior year of high school, he submitted some cartoons to the editors of his class yearbook. Almost predictably
Sparky's drawings were rejected.

While the young man had stoically rationalized virtually
all of his failures theretofore, he was rather hurt by the general ignorance of what he believed was his one natural talent.
In fact, he was so convinced of his artistic ability that he decided to become a professional artist.

Upon graduating high school, he wrote a letter to Walt
Disney Studios, a letter indicating his qualifications to become a cartoonist for Disney.

Shortly he received an answer, a form letter requesting
that he send some examples of his artwork. Subject matter
was suggested. For instance, a Disney cartoon character "re-
pairing" a clock by shoveling the springs and gears back inside.

Sparky drew the proposed cartoon scene. He spent a great
deal of time on that and the other drawings. A job with Disney would be impressive, and there were many doubters to
impress.

Sparky mailed the form and his drawings to Disney Studios.

Sparky waited.

And one day the reply came. . . .

It was another form letter, very politely composed. It said
that Disney Studios hired only the very finest artists, even for
their routine background work. It had been determined from
the drawings which Sparky had submitted—that he was *not*
one of the very finest artists.

In other words, he did not get the job.

I think deep down Sparky expected to be rejected. He had
always been a loser, and this was simply one more loss.

So you know what Sparky did? He wrote his autobiogra-
phy in *cartoons*. He described his childhood self, the little-
boy loser, the chronic underachiever, in a cartoon character
the whole world now knows.

For the boy who failed the entire eighth grade, the young artist whose work was rejected not only by Walt Disney Studios but his own high school yearbook, that young man was "Sparky" Charles Monroe Schulz.

He created the "Peanuts" comic strip and the little cartoon boy whose kite would never fly—Charlie Brown.

38. Genuine as a Three-Dollar Bill

I'M GOING TO TEST your knowledge of United States currency.

Whose face appears on the one-dollar bill?

Correct. Washington.

And on the five-dollar bill?

Right again. Lincoln.

How about the ten?

Hamilton.

And the twenty?

Jackson.

Now it gets tougher. Who is depicted on the fifty-dollar bill?

Ulysses Grant.

And on the one-hundred-dollar bill?

Ben Franklin.

And yes, there are higher denominations of U.S. paper currency, although federal regulations demand that should a bank come into possession of such currency, the bill or bills must be returned to the regional Federal Reserve bank. While such paper money is technically "out of circulation," it is still legal tender. Try to change one of these bills at a bank, however, and it—and perhaps you as well—will be examined stem to stern.

On the five-hundred-dollar bill there is a picture of President William McKinley.

On the one-thousand-dollar bill, President Grover Cleveland.

On the five-thousand-dollar bill, President James Madison.

On the ten-thousand-dollar bill, nineteenth-century U.S. Supreme Court Chief Justice Salmon Chase.

And finally, the one-hundred-thousand-dollar bill. The highest-ever denomination of United States currency. Thereon is depicted President Woodrow Wilson.

But we're not finished.

As any racetrack habitué might inform you, there is also a two-dollar bill. On this otherwise seldom seen yet no less legal tender, one finds the picture of Thomas Jefferson.

And there is one more bill we have overlooked: the *three*-dollar bill.

Genuine American currency, despite the threadbare simile which implies nothing could be phonier.

Never in a million years would you guess who is depicted on the three-dollar bill, so I'd better tell you THE REST OF THE STORY.

Once upon a time, banks all over the country issued their own currency. Even after the National Bank Act of 1863 imposed a 10 percent tax on such notes, many banks continued to make their own money.

By 1935, the national banks had transferred this power to the Federal Reserve. Yet throughout most of this nation's history, bank-issued currency, now relegated to myriad numismatic collections, was as legal a tender as any.

The banks issued every denomination of paper money now in circulation, plus one: the three-dollar bill.

Specific designs varied from bank to bank. But one design was used more than any other.

That preeminent picture was, as on current currency, of someone. Someone you've known all your life.

He appeared on the three-dollar bills issued by the Howard Banking Company of Boston and the Central Bank of Troy and the Pittsfield Bank and the White Mountain Bank—and by one Manhattan bank bearing the name of the man on the three-dollar bill: the Saint Nicholas Bank of New York City.

And yes, I do mean to tell you that the person whose image was once absolutely lawfully engraved on the dead-serious 100 percent legitimate three-dollar bill—was *Santa Claus.*

39. Blissful Dreams

GEORGE COOPER.

. Look him up.

You'll find him under "poetry" or "songwriting." Either heading. His poetry provided the lyrics for dozens of songs.

There's a story about George Cooper you'll be interested in, a story that appears in a number of reference sources, a story about George's "one and only love."

George had been married less than a year when his lovely young bride died. Deeply grieved, he nevertheless bravely continued with his profession as a poet.

Years passed, and still he was haunted by the memory of his dearly departed wife.

Fifteen years after her death, George was compelled to interpret that memory in verse.

The verse was sold to composer Henry Tucker for five dollars, and the song that resulted became an everlasting monument to the woman whom fate had so cruelly taken from poet George Cooper.

That is the story as history books tell it and retell it.

According to a number of historical references, George Cooper's young bride died, and fifteen years later he immortalized her in the lyrics of a song.

The contention is that this young lady was the only woman in Cooper's life.

"His only love . . ."

"He never loved again. . . ."

Not to say that is impossible. It is merely a sweeping state-ment which, incidentally, is easily proved false.

George was married at the age of thirty-seven to a woman who bore him two sons and a daughter, a woman whose name is *not* the same as the lady he mentions in the song.

Further . . .

The often-repeated story claims Cooper wrote the lyrics to that song fifteen years after his bride had passed away. But George wrote the lyrics in 1869, age twenty-nine. That would make him a widower at fourteen! Again, not impossible. But *very* unlikely.

The bottom line is this.

Two highly respected popular-music historians, Russ San-jek and Fletcher Hodges, agree that the heart-strumming story of George Cooper and his dearly departed bride is al-most certainly false—was probably contrived by Cooper him-self for the purpose of generating interest in his poetry.

That's not all.

Mr. Hodges says there is evidence that poet George Cooper, in his old age, actually began to believe the story, began to fall in love with the fictitious mystery lady he made famous when he wrote:

> Oh Genevieve, sweet Genevieve,
> The days may come, the days may go,
> But still the hands of mem'ry weave
> The blissful dreams of long ago.

Now you know THE REST OF THE STORY.

40. John Cheese

THEY WERE THE FIRST minority on Manhattan. They were disliked and distrusted. They were the objects of unflattering humor. They were called all sorts of names, one so insulting they adopted it into their own native language.

They were the Holland Dutch.

The Dutch were there first, you know. It was Dutchman Peter Minuit who purchased Manhattan from the Indians in 1626. The settlement was called New Amsterdam and would become the seat of government for the colony of New Netherland.

The Dutch West India Company paid little attention to the settlers at first. For three years New Amsterdam attracted a rough bunch—privateers, smugglers, and so on.

The first organized social system in the colony was a kind of feudalism. Huge estates with dozens of tenant families on each. The early governors and councils ruled without popular assemblies and were renowned for their harshness.

Meanwhile, the British were growing perturbed over the presence of New Netherland, an obtrusive interruption in the sequence of their coastal possessions. In 1664, a small English naval force set out to capture the Dutch colony. The Dutch surrendered without firing a shot.

Seven thousand of them decided to accept British rule in order to keep their homes. For a while Anglo-Dutch relations were not bad. Yet as hostilities developed between the respective motherlands, the English inhabitants of the colony now known as New York grew increasingly unfriendly toward the Dutch minority.

First privately, ultimately publicly, the British New Yorkers began making fun. Anything negative was automatically characterized as being "Dutch."

Many related phrases remain a part of our vernacular: anyone who is stern and hypercritical we still call a "Dutch uncle."

A "Dutch treat," of course, is no treat at all.

Getting into trouble we often refer to as "getting into Dutch."

The slurs don't stop there. . . .

"Dutch widow" once meant prostitute.

Frogs used to be called "Dutch nightingales."

One who was said to have taken the "Dutch route" had killed himself.

"Dutch defense" was surrender.

"Dutch praise" was condemnation.

"Dutch courage" was extracted from a bottle.

And a "Dutch medley"? That's when everyone sings a different tune—simultaneously.

And the list goes on.

But there was one epithet to which the Dutch themselves particularly objected. You know how ethnic slurs often reflect the foods with which a minority may be identified? Well, the Dutch were supposedly characteristically fond of cheese. So the English began referring to Dutchmen as "John Cheese." That upset the Dutch so much that they eventually turned the nasty nickname around, actually calling Englishmen "John Cheese."

In the language of the Netherlands, naturally.

It was that epithet which made the most indelible impression of all.

In time the world would forget that a hangover was once defined as "Dutchman's headache," and that "Dutch gold" meant the phony stuff.

What we remember is the unflattering term "John Cheese," a label the Dutch ultimately laid on us. The way they said it was *Jan Kees*.
You know.
Yankees.
Now you know THE REST OF THE STORY.

41. We Salute You!

BOB AWAKENED TREMBLING from a dream, a dream that had seemed more vivid than the morning sunlight in his eyes, a dream of the day which now lay before him—a dream of his own death.

Bob accepted the dream as a premonition, and he brooded over it for hours, telling no one. Who among his friends in Oxford, Maryland, would believe such nonsense? That he, Bob, a successful merchant and one of the best-loved men in the colonies, was about to be shot and killed!

Bob resolved not to leave the house that day. Then he remembered a business obligation: one of his ships had arrived in port, and the captain of that vessel had invited Bob aboard for an afternoon dinner party.

It was customary in 1750 for the captain of a merchant ship to entertain the consignee before setting sail again. Bob would attempt to break that tradition just this once.

He summoned Captain Mathews and apologized personally for his unwillingness to attend the shipboard celebration. Bob even told the captain about his dream, confessing his fear that he would be shot and killed if he ventured out that day.

At this point, history itself asks a question. We know that Bob changed his mind and decided to attend the captain's party—but we don't know why. One scholar suggests that Captain Mathews became indignant at the merchant's refusal, and that Bob then reaccepted the captain's invitation to preserve their good business relationship.

More likely, however, the captain assured Bob he would

be safe—the vessel was armed for defense, after all—and Bob, now slightly embarrassed that he had taken a mere dream so seriously, told the captain he would be on board at the appointed time.

What you are about to read we know for sure. That afternoon Bob went down to the dock with Captain Mathews, boarded a small vessel propelled by oars and sails, and set out for the big merchant ship which was moored farther down the bay.

Aboard the merchant ship Bob was wined and dined, was entertained by pipes and dancing sailors. Finally Bob was willing to admit that dreams were only dreams, and that life was well worth living in spite of them.

It was still light when he boarded the small sailing vessel for his return to Oxford. Captain Mathews would escort him home.

Bob, the Maryland merchant, was Robert Morris, Sr. His son, Robert, Jr., was in that summer of 1750 a boy of sixteen. You should know him.

Robert Morris, Jr., was a signer of the Declaration of Independence, a wealthy patriot who has been called the financier of the American Revolution. His money saved our government from bankruptcy. His money sent George Washington to Yorktown to force the surrender of General Cornwallis.

The foundation upon which Robert Morris, Jr., built his fortune was seven thousand dollars that he inherited from his father, the beloved Maryland merchant you've already met, the man who dreamed of his own doom.

For Robert Morris, Sr., really did lose his life that summer day in 1750. He really was shot and killed.

It happened after he left the merchant ship and boarded the small ship-to-shore vessel. It happened as he was sailing away.

For there was another eighteenth-century tradition.

On departing a merchant ship, the merchant consignee was always saluted by the ship's cannon.

Robert Morris, Sr., age thirty-nine, had not quite sailed beyond the cannon's range.

His own ship saluted him to death!

Now you know THE REST OF THE STORY.

42. From Afar

THERE IS AN ELUSIVE, illusory love in the life of comic-strip character Charlie Brown. She is "the little red-haired girl." She is Charlie Brown's ideal, the perfection of which all else falls short. But either circumstances or the little boy's own shyness perpetually stands in the way of their romance.

Once upon a time, there was a Charlie Brown. Only his "little red-haired girl" had golden curls and smiling, beguiling blue eyes.

The real-life little boy—his name was Harry—met this devastating creature in Sunday school when he and she were six. He learned her name, Elizabeth Virginia Wallace. He would not use it for five years. So in awe was he of this vision of loveliness that for five years he could not summon the courage to speak to her.

As the youngsters grew up, it became apparent that pretty Miss Wallace was the more athletically inclined of the two. A tomboy is what she was. Superlative in sports. The only girl in town who could whistle through her teeth.

Little Harry admired her greatly for it. Still he worshipped from afar. He might have been intimidated by her family's affluence or by her grandfather's imposing community-pillar status—but he was not. He was merely gloriously overwhelmed by *her*, as it seemed he would always be.

In high school Harry continued to daydream about lovely Elizabeth Wallace, although by then he had managed to make occasional contact. He had once even walked Elizabeth home from school, carrying her books, which the love-struck boy considered a major triumph. He wrote songs for her and, doubtless, poetry.

Of course, Harry was not her only admirer. Elizabeth had more prospective boyfriends than all the other girls in school put together. How might she, then, have noticed that one boy in particular with room in his heart only for her?

At the age of nineteen, the high-spirited, strong-willed young lady was dealt a deflating blow. Her forty-three-year-old father, in a despondent swoon, committed suicide. Following the tragedy, Elizabeth moved into her grandfather's mansion at 219 North Delaware and from there to an exclusive finishing school.

While Elizabeth was winning shot-put contests and serving as her school basketball team's star forward, Harry remained home and true to her memory, earning modest wages as a local bank clerk.

It is incredible that these two utterly dissimilar people ever got together. Even after Elizabeth's graduation had put the distractions of education behind her, there was still very little foundation for a relationship with Harry. She liked fishing and ice skating and tennis and dancing and card games and ball games and all the activities by which Harry was completely bored.

To Elizabeth's grandparents, he was something less than a suitable suitor. No money, no college education, apparently no future, a thoroughly unpromising prospect for a husband. But there was one thing on which the young lady's family and friends had not counted: the young man loved her deeply, had placed her on a pedestal at the age of six in Sunday school and simply refused to let her down.

If a success was what Elizabeth's mother and grandparents wanted for her, then he would become successful. He would court the girl of his dreams until she gave in, and she did give in and marry him—at thirty-five!

Yes, they lived happily ever after. Shared an infinite affection and a marvelous sense of humor, it is said. And by the way, the path of achievement upon which Harry had originally set out to impress Elizabeth's family eventually led him all the way.

For this was the Independence, Missouri, courtship of Harry and Bess Truman.

Now you know THE REST OF THE STORY.

43. The Remains of General Santa Anna

OF ALL THE DAYS in all the year 1842, one day would live longest in the memories of the Mexican people.

That day was September 27, the day they exhumed the remains of General Antonio López de Santa Anna.

You remember General Santa Anna. He was the so-and-so who stormed the Alamo.

September 27, 1842, the remains of this colorful national leader were dug up at Manga de Clavo. Those remains, contained in an urn, were born majestically through the streets of Mexico City.

It was a ceremony of homage to Santa Anna, the man who had declared himself "Serene Highness" of his country.

The solemn procession was comprised of cavalry, infantry, artillery, cadets from the military academy at Chapultepec—a grand escort to the cemetery of Santa Paula, where the urn was to be reinterred.

At the new grave site, national dignitaries gave speeches, recited poems. Flags waved. Cannon saluted. Those in attendance were irresistibly reminded of that peculiar international conflict back in 1838.

History books would call it the "Pastry War."

It all started in the city of Veracruz on the east coast of Mexico, in a pastry shop owned by a Frenchman. One night several Mexican army officers paid the French baker a visit, locked him in the back room of his shop, and began eating all his pastries. When at last he was freed, the angry baker sued the Mexican government. The government ignored him. That brought the French fleet to the port of Veracruz, and the Mexican defenders surrendered. Except for General Santa Anna.

General Santa Anna mounted his steed, rode off down the shoreline, shouting at the French fleet as it was sailing away victorious.

The French admiral was amused by the ranting Santa Anna. Then, when the ranting grew boring, the departing admiral fired a cannon shot at the general.

It is doubtful that the admiral ever expected to hit his target, yet in this he underestimated the accuracy of his ship's artillery.

General Santa Anna was hit by the French cannonball. He dictated a fifteen-page "deathbed message" to the Mexican people as aides knelt weeping at his side.

It was surely the most spectacular military burial the citizens of Veracruz had ever seen. The general's remains were laid to rest on a hilltop overlooking the city. And in September 1842, the splendid reinterment in Mexico City took place.

And did I mention that General Santa Anna died in 1876?

You see, the general rose from his "deathbed" in 1838, but he recovered minus a leg. The French admiral had shot off one of Santa Anna's legs!

It was the general's separated *limb* which was buried with honors at Veracruz, and four years later in Mexico City.

Thirty-four years more would pass before Santa Anna got around to dying. By then the Mexican people were so sick of him that few even noticed.

In fact, the shallow, bombastic, egotistical Santa Anna may have been the only man in history whose leg received a better funeral than the rest of him!

Now you know THE REST OF THE STORY.

44. For Carrie's One True Love

CARRIE BOND might have told you that life without love is hard, also that one true love can make life a paradise.

Carrie might have told you that.

And, in a way, she did.

She was born Carrie Jacobs, the only child of a prosperous Wisconsin businessman.

When Carrie was severely burned at the age of seven, the family hoped that life's cruelest blow was behind her. It was only the first in a succession of hard knocks.

She was ten when her daddy's business went bankrupt. Some said the strain was too much for him. In weeks he was dead. Carrie and her mother managed as best they could.

The Christmas Day of her eighteenth year, Carrie married. The groom's name was Ed Smith, and he worked in a men's clothing store.

I don't know that Carrie "had to marry." Perhaps the child born almost precisely seven months after the wedding was premature. It was whispered, however, that the marriage of Carrie and Ed was "not right from the beginning." Indeed, they were separated before their son was six and divorced the following year.

Not long after the divorce, Carrie, still in her mid-twenties, became reacquainted with a childhood friend. He was Frank Lewis Bond, by then an established, respected physician. They were married June 10, 1889, and theirs was to be the love of Carrie's life.

One day Frank recalled that Carrie had taken piano lessons as a young girl, and he asked his bride to play something for him. She did. And when she had finished, Frank made Carrie promise never to give up her music. "You are too talented!" he declared, and his praise was more than adequate inspiration for Carrie to continue practicing.

Of course, that was the way Frank was. He made Carrie feel special in all ways. More important, his love was Carrie's haven from the world and its trouble. All the unhappiness she had known, her childhood anguish and failed first marriage, all that was forgotten during the years she and Frank Bond were as one. But not even this seemingly unassailable joy was to last.

In 1893, a national depression. Frank's finances collapsed. Slowly the grim shadow of her father's final despair was cast once more over Carrie's life. Frank assured his wife that he was strong, that *they* were strong, and that they would see this hardship through.

The confident words had a hollow ring. In fact, Frank's promise would not be kept. His financial adversity continued, and in 1895 he died suddenly.

Rich or poor, Carrie had been more than happy with Frank at her side. Now that blissful light was extinguished forever. How could Carrie go on?

Then she remembered an earlier promise to Frank: She must never give up her music. Although impoverished, she would struggle to get by any way she could—renting rooms, painting chinaware. But she would continue to play the piano and to write songs, and maybe someday someone might even publish her work.

One day, someone did.

Carrie Jacobs Bond died in 1946, age eighty-four, after four decades of wealth and world fame. We have always known the words and music that made her famous. Now we know Dr. Frank Bond, Carrie's one true love, the man who encouraged her music, the gentle lover who made the world go away.

It was for him that Carrie wrote:

> I love you truly, truly dear!
> Life with its sorrow, life with its tear
> Fades into dreams when I feel you are near,
> For I love you truly, truly dear!

You've always known that song. Only now you know THE REST OF THE STORY.

45. How the Defenders Held Out on Bataan

THE BATAAN PENINSULA lies west of Manila Bay in the Philippines. It is familiar worldwide because of something that happened there during World War II.

For it was only hours after the attack on Pearl Harbor that the Japanese went after the Philippine Islands. They moved so swiftly and decisively that American and Filipino troops were forced to retreat into a defense zone: the Bataan peninsula.

Depot areas were quickly constructed in the interior. Docks were developed along the peninsular coast. In the north, defense lines were designated. And then a fundamental strategy was conceived.

The Americans and Filipinos would stage a heavy resistance, forcing the Japanese aggressors to concentrate their troops. Then slowly, almost imperceptibly, the defenders would withdraw. But as the Japanese advanced, they would run into every booby trap American demolition engineers could devise.

These tactics would be repeated over and over. And they accomplished their primary purpose: to consume time.

It is for this that Bataan is famous.

History records that after a gallant ninety-eight-day stand against impossible odds, the American and Filipino defenders surrendered to the Japanese. The cruelty of the enemy during and after the notorious "death march" to the prison camps will perhaps never be forgotten. But the real triumph of the defenders of Bataan was that they wasted so much of the enemy's valuable time. They stalled so long, forcing the Japanese to fight ten times harder than they might otherwise have had to, that the soldiers of the Rising Sun never caught up, never got back on their wartime timetable. Because of that magnificent holdout on Bataan, the Japanese military effort in the South Pacific never got back on schedule.

One Japanese historical record relates: "There was an influence, a spiritual influence, exerted by the resistance on Bataan. Not only did the Japanese at home worry about the length of the period of resistance on Bataan, but it served to indicate to the Filipinos that the Americans had not deserted them and would continue to try to assist them."

During that brave stand of almost a hundred days, the Allies were able to organize the defense of Australia and other vital areas in the Southwest Pacific.

Even at that, because the Allies were committed to "get Hitler first," they would not provide the Bataan defenders with all the supplies and reinforcements and troop replacements and air support they so badly needed.

Said General MacArthur of his heroic soldiers on Bataan: "My heart ached as I saw my men slowly wasting away. Their clothes hung on them like tattered rags. Their bare feet stuck out in silent protest. Their long bedraggled hair framed gaunt bloodless faces . . . They cursed the enemy and in the same breath cursed and reviled the United States . . ."

But they hung on. They continued to fight. For ninety-eight days. And until now, few knew THE REST OF THE STORY.

For, shortly before the beginning of the war, General MacArthur's quartermaster put in an order for some fuel containers, eighteen thousand empty fifty-five-gallon oil drums.

I say *empty* drums. There was already plenty of fuel stored throughout the Philippines.

But someone fouled up the order for those fuel containers, sent eighteen thousand fifty-five-gallon drums *full of gasoline.*

Thus was a million gallons of then unwanted, unneeded

fuel sent across the bay to an out-of-the-way storage dump—on the peninsula of Battan.

It was that fuel which fueled the tanks and the transports and the tractors and the generators, the war machinery of the Bataan defenders. And conserving as best they could for almost a hundred precious, bloody days, they at last ran out of the gas—that nobody ordered.

46. The Prize

THERE IS NO human relationship quite like that of a man and his mother. When it comes to her son, a mother's faith is eternal.

Thelma Toole believed in her son John even when he did not.

In his early teens John began writing a book, completed it in the sixties while he was in the army. When John got out of the army, it was to discover that no one was interested in what he had written.

Incidentally, this book was about a man with a Middle Ages mentality trapped in present-day New Orleans.

One by one, the publishers said: "Thanks, but no thanks. . . ."

John Toole went back to school. Tulane. Then a master's at Columbia.

It was John's mother who continually encouraged him to market that book. "It's a great book!" she insisted. So John would send the manuscript out again and again, until one day in 1969 he gave up in despair.

John's mother did not give up. She mailed, sometimes even hand-delivered, her son's manuscript to another publisher, then another—six, seven, eight publishers.

Their answers were all approximately the same. "Thanks, but there is no present market . . ."

Then Mrs. Toole heard that Louisiana State University was going into the book-publishing business. Perhaps those people would appreciate a New Orleans story!

They did.

They published the book called *Confederacy of Dunces*, hoping perhaps to sell enough copies to break even.

Instead, they sold forty thousand hardback copies. The book became a best-seller on a dozen lists, was cited by several critics as the year's best.

Another publisher bid for and was awarded paperback rights. The manuscript nobody wanted, the sensitive writing by an author whose genius was appreciated only by his mother, that book, in April of 1981, was awarded the prestigious Pulitzer Prize for fiction. With that distinction goes the fame, fortune, and recognition which the author had sought, yet had failed to find.

There are few more profound utterances than this from the lips of a country parson named Frank Clark: "A lot of impulsive mistakes are made by people who simply aren't willing to stay bored a little longer."

I mentioned, did I not, that John Toole sought to interest eight different publishers in his novel before he finally gave up in 1969?

Since then, it had been his mother who persisted until the book was accepted.

And one thing more.

It was his mother who accepted the 1981 Pulitzer Prize in John's name.

For John Toole, frustrated by repeated rejections, despondent because he considered himself a failure, put a pistol to his head in 1969 and ended his life at thirty-two years.

He gave up on this world, believing it had given up on him.

You know one person who did not.

Because now you know THE REST OF THE STORY.

47. The Entertainers

TODAY, PUBLIC WELFARE and health care are considered by many to be "basic human rights." And Ben Franklin is spinning in his grave. . . .

Ben was basically down on charitable institutions. He once observed that offering the poor "a dependence on anything for support . . . besides industry and frugality during youth and health, tends to flatter our natural indolence, to encourage idleness and prodigality, and thereby promote and increase poverty, the very evil it was intended to cure, thus multiplying beggars instead of diminishing them."

Then one day a friend talked Ben into changing his mind.

The friend's name was Thomas Bond, and he hoped to establish a hospital in Philadelphia to provide health care for the poor. The problem was that without the endorsement of Ben Franklin, subscribers were virtually impossible to find.

Tom appealed to Ben, and Ben agreed to support the project; and thus was founded Philadelphia Hospital—the first hospital in America.

Mid-eighteenth century, the plague of the American colonies was mental illness. There was an alarming increase in its incidence about the time Dr. Thomas Bond was planning to build his hospital.

The institution opened its doors early in 1752, and the mentally ill comprised a large percentage of the early admissions. Because those with mental disorders tended to stay sick longer than those with physical disorders, administrators were greatly concerned that Philadelphia Hospital might become primarily an insane asylum. Many of the mentally disturbed who checked in were to remain for years, never to check out. And the facility was phenomenally ill prepared for some of the cases it accepted.

Two patients—one Jonathan Jones and another, Charles Jenkins—could not be held, even by the iron bars on their respective cells. After at least seven escapes each, a blacksmith was summoned to reinforce the cell bars of Jones and Jenkins. Yet even the blacksmith underestimated the potential physical strength of the violently insane. Charles Jenkins continued to escape.

One escapee, a former seaman named Thomas Perrine, fled his basement cell and ran through the hospital, finally seeking refuge in the cupola. He had long fingernails, long matted hair and beard, and he loomed like a giant bird on his towering perch. All attempts to get him down were unsuccessful, and so the staff just left him up there, sent up his bedding and food, and there he died almost ten years later.

For others the end came more swiftly. Some jumped from the roof. At least one unhappy patient hanged himself.

The reason we know so much about what happened is that the hospital kept such accurate records. And also that there were so many observers.

You may have wondered what the colonists did for entertainment two centuries before television.

Originally, admission was free. Later, the general public was admitted at four cents a head. It was difficult, usually impossible, to screen the cruel from the crowds. There was much laughing and taunting. Some even poked sticks through the bars at the cowering patients.

The history books tell us that America's first zoo opened in Philadelphia in 1874.

You know that it was in fact 122 years earlier, and that the "animals" were *people*. Because now you know THE REST OF THE STORY.

48. The Genius of Karl Kroyer

In 1964, THE FREIGHTER *Al Kuwait,* all twenty-seven hundred tons of her, capsized and sank to the bottom of Kuwait Harbor. That nation's government might have left her there had she not been carrying a cargo of six thousand sheep!

Fear was that the rotting carcasses would poison the harbor. So the shipping company would be required to clean up its mess.

But no one knew how.

Neither the Kuwaiti government nor the shipping company had any idea of how to recover those thousands of dead sheep from the bottom of the harbor.

Then someone remembered Karl Kroyer.

A Danish inventor. A genius, some said. His inventions had earned him a million dollars many times over—his bicycle-wheel-rim linings and his various kitchen appliances and his nonskid highway surfacing and all the other profitable patentables on which his international reputation rested.

So the Kuwaiti ship owners called Karl Kroyer.

No way to conduct the cleanup operation underwater, Karl decided. The freighter would first have to be raised to the surface.

The ship owners agreed.

But they had tried all the conventional methods of ship raising, and all had failed.

Karl said he would think about it. The Kuwaitis would hear from him soon.

They did.

Karl dispatched a small vessel to Kuwait Harbor, armed with a long injector hose and 30 *billion* pea-sized polystyrene pellets. If hollow, air-sealed, superbuoyant plastic balls could be injected into the sunken ship's hull, the ship itself would become buoyant and float to the surface.

Karl Kroyer's divers descended into Kuwait Harbor, and they carried out his instructions. The plan worked. The freighter was raised to an even keel. Mission accomplished.

Karl's fee was a handsome although not unreasonable $186,000.

And word got around.

Off the coast of Greenland, a similar situation with a sunken steamer. The shipowners called Karl Kroyer. The vessel was raised successfully.

Again, off Scotland, same situation. Kroyer was commissioned and came to the rescue.

Finally, Van Den Tak of Holland, Europe's biggest ship-salvage company, joined forces with inventor Kroyer. And today polystyrene pellets are used routinely to raise sunken ships which could not have been recovered two decades ago.

Karl Kroyer might really have cashed in had he been able to patent his process. Yet he could not obtain a patent for a concept that was already in existence.

For Karl had borrowed the hollow plastic pellet idea. He had read about it in a magazine. He had read about a sunken yacht which had been raised to the surface by being stuffed full of Ping-Pong balls!

Genius inventor-engineer Karl Kroyer remembered reading about that operation in a 1949 publication.

A comic book.

The genius behind the genius of Karl Kroyer was Walt Disney's Donald Duck.

Now you know THE REST OF THE STORY.

49. The Reluctant Hangman

It is the night of September 5, 1872, and you are standing at the bedside of a sleepless man.

For him this is one in a succession of all-but-sleepless nights, although tonight he is particularly in anguish.

Tomorrow he must do the unimaginable. Tomorrow he personally will end a man's life.

Meet Stephen, sheriff of Erie County, New York.

He is a good man. A fair man. A man with a reverence for responsibility. But will his conscience permit him to meet this one responsibility, now only hours away?

For as sheriff he must also serve as county executioner— as hangman! He, personally, must pull the trapdoor lever. In Erie County, that is the Law.

So there in the stillness, in the dark, Sheriff Stephen tosses and turns. His mind wanders to another restless soul, the condemned man.

Not the sort you would want to spare, really. Fellow named Patrick Morrissey. He had stabbed his own mother to death in a drunken rage.

Stephen, a believer in capital punishment, would not mind *sending* that man to the gallows. But could he actually, physically, with his own hand, trip the mechanism that would yank the world out from under a living human being?

Just how merciful is this execution the sheriff is duty-bound to perform? Will the prisoner's demise be swift, or will he linger between life and death in agony?

In the middle of one restless night recently past, Stephen

had awakened a physician friend from a sound sleep simply to ask how a hangman might dispatch his victim painlessly.

Stephen even sought his mother's counsel, asking her if he should proceed with this deed. Sympathetically she reminded her son of the loophole, the provision of county law that legally the sheriff could delegate the dirty work to a deputy with an attached fee of ten dollars.

But here in the quiet darkness, on the eve of the execution, Stephen remembers his answer to his mother: He could never ask another man to do that which he could not bring himself to do. It all came down to that.

The following day, September 6, 1872, within the walls of the county jailyard at fourteen minutes past high noon, Buffalo's first execution in more than six years was accomplished.

Sheriff Stephen pulled the fatal lever himself.

The county records of New York's Erie County show that on January 1, 1871, a man named Stephen became sheriff, and that on September 6 of the following year he accepted the role of executioner, a sworn responsibility of his public office.

By county law, he, Stephen, was required to release the gallows trapdoor by his own hand.

You have watched Stephen wrestle with his conscience. You now know the personal anguish he endured. That inner strength he summoned would continue to serve him, even as he one day accepted this nation's most awe-inspiring responsibility.

Stephen, the sheriff and reluctant hangman of Erie County, became President Stephen Grover Cleveland.

Now you know THE REST OF THE STORY.

50. They Were Very Special Songs

WHEN COUNTRY SINGER Hank Williams was found dead in the backseat of his Cadillac, his fans were sure it was the drugs and the booze. Hank was being chauffeur-driven to an engagement in Canton, Ohio. During a stop in West Virginia, the chauffeur discovered him. The cause of death was officially recorded as a heart attack. He was twenty-nine.

If you remember Hank Williams, you remember best his song "Your Cheatin' Heart." But there was another song, his most popular at the time of his death. A very special song.

Rhythm-and-blues singer Chuck Willis was about Hank Williams' age when he, Willis, died six years later in 1958. Like Williams, Willis died in an automobile, although the usual way. A car wreck near Atlanta, Georgia.

Before his death, Chuck Willis was hailed in the trades as one of the ten most important rhythm-and-blues performers ever. Yet beyond the realm of personal taste, it would be difficult to identify him with any one particular song. There were two particularly popular ones at the time of his death. Two very special songs.

Also, there was Buddy Holly. Songwriter Don McLean once referred to that day as "the day the music died," February 3, 1959, when Buddy Holly's plane went down.

Holly, twenty years young, took two other big-name rock-and-rollers with him: Ritchie Valens and J. P. Richardson, otherwise known as the "Big Bopper."

The three were touring together, were en route to another

booking when their light plane crashed in a field near Mason City, Iowa.

Ultimately it was Holly's death which was most keenly felt among the enthusiasts of rock and roll.

He is remembered for so many songs—"Peggy Sue," "That'll Be the Day," "Early in the Morning," "Think It Over," "Fool's Paradise," "Heartbeat"—and yet there was one very special song, and that one was among his very last.

Singer-songwriter Eddie Cochran died a year later in April of 1960. He was twenty-one, was in fact one month younger than colleague Buddy Holly.

Like Hank Williams, rock singer Cochran was chauffeured to the Great Beyond. His triumphant European tour had ended in London, and he was eager to return to California for a rest. On the way to the airport, one of the limousine tires blew out, the driver lost control, and the limousine slammed into a lamp post. Multiple head injuries killed Cochran.

He had only begun to enjoy the phenomenal popularity of one of his recordings. A very special song.

They were all very special songs. Those that had met with such success at the tragic terminations of Hank Williams' career and Chuck Willis' career and Buddy Holly's career and Eddie Cochran's career.

For if the future sometimes casts a shadow, it could have been no more evident than when Hank Williams sang "I'll Never Get Out of This World Alive" and died. And when Chuck Willis sang "Hang Up My Rock and Roll Shoes" and "What Am I Living For?" and died. And when Buddy Holly sang "It Doesn't Matter Anymore" and died. And when Eddie Cochran sang "Three Steps to Heaven" and died.

Of course, you remember John Lennon.

His most popular new song at the time of his death, his last recording, was "Starting Over."

Now you know THE REST OF THE STORY.

51. We Never Sleep

ALLAN WAS A Chartist.

Perhaps I'd better explain.

Chartism was a movement for democratic social and political reform, the first nationwide working-class movement in Great Britain. It took place between 1836 and 1848, was named after something called the People's Charter. The Chartists promoted their cause vociferously, sometimes violently.

And Allan was a Chartist. A rabble-rouser, according to the king.

Indeed, Allan had participated in Chartist riots in Glasgow. A police sergeant was wounded. Now the police were looking for Allan. There was even a price on his head.

Allan was an outlaw.

In the winter of 1842 the authorities thought they had him trapped. They went to the tenement house where he was last seen. But the young Scot had fled.

For months thereafter, Chartist comrades hid him in attics and secret rooms.

Early in March it was arranged that Allan's sweetheart, Joan, be brought to him. Allan explained that he would have to leave for America soon, make a fresh start. But how lonesome his exile would be without the girl he loved!

Joan accepted Allan's proposal, and they were married secretly on the thirteenth.

Four weeks later, they were smuggled aboard a ship bound for the New World.

This was only the beginning of an adventure the young outlaw and his bride would never forget.

After a stormy passage, their ship struck a rock and sank off the coast of Nova Scotia. Allan and Joan made it to shore in a lifeboat.

By May they had reached Montreal, where Allan, a barrelmaker by trade, managed to get a temporary job making beer barrels.

Eventually the couple settled in Dundee, Illinois, where Allan opened his own shop. What happened then is THE REST OF THE STORY.

Allan had heard that there was a gang of counterfeiters at large. When he, Allan, spied the gang's forest hideout, he ran and told the local sheriff. The sheriff said he would need assistance in the capture. Allan was temporarily deputized. I say temporarily. And yet from that day until the last day of his life, Allan, a wanted man in his own country, a young fugitive with a price on his head, would pursue a career in law enforcement. Once an outlaw; now and forever after, a lawman.

Kane County Sheriff's Office.

Chicago Police Department.

Finally, his own private-detective agency with offices in Chicago and New York and Philadelphia.

While similar agencies of that era had grimy reputations, Allan's organization was prestigious. He refused to investigate the sexual morals of otherwise law-abiding citizens. He refused to regulate fees on a basis proportional to the amount of money recovered in a theft.

Soon Allan and the super crime-busters serving under him were known nationwide as the best of the good guys.

It was Allan and his investigators who uncovered an early plot to assassinate President Lincoln, and who first proposed the organization of a national secret service.

Some called Allan's transformation from outlaw to lawman remarkable, but then maybe law enforcement was in his blood.

Remember the police sergeant back in Glasgow, the one who was wounded in the Chartist riots? He was rioter Chartist Allan's *father.*

And one thing more—the motto of Allan's always-vigilant detective agency was "We Never Sleep." The graphic design which always appeared above that slogan was an open, alert human eye.

For that reason we still call private investigators "private eyes."

We still refer, if unwittingly, to the sign above the door of the detective agency that would bear Allan's name thenceforth, the name of the Scottish policeman's son, the young man with a price on his head, the fugitive from justice who was destined to make justice his life—Allan *Pinkerton.*

52. The Loving Hands

CHARLES FISK MAKES pipe organs for churches and universities. He has been called "the most influential American organ builder of the twentieth century." A man of rare good fortune in that he is doing for money what he would do for nothing. His profession is the pursuit of his dreams.

To this he owes a nightmare, and that is THE REST OF THE STORY.

Charles Fisk grew up in Cambridge, Massachusetts. His teenage reputation was that of an electronics wizard. He was building tube amplifiers before there was such a term as "high fidelity."

Later Charles would attend Harvard and Stanford. It was at Stanford where he realized he could no longer cope with the nightmare, and where he decided upon the career for which he is now famous.

In 1954 he left the university to apprentice under renowned organ maker Walter Holtkamp. Within eighteen months, Fisk had earned a partnership in the Andover Organ Company.

By 1959 he owned that company.

By 1962 he had moved to Gloucester, Massachusetts, as C. B. Fisk, Incorporated.

Long before, Charles had abandoned the electronic wizardry which had made him talk-of-the-town in his teen years. Indeed, there was something decidedly antitechnological in the Charles Fisk approach to organ making.

First, all Fisk organs are "tracker" organs. No electronics.

Simply woods and rods and wires, as one might discover in a pipe organ centuries old. Charles even quarreled with that one lonesome twentieth-century touch found in all modern trackers: the electric-blower motor!

Fisk understood that nobody wanted to stand around in the church basement pumping organ bellows nowadays. He also understood that the organs of old rendered a slightly irregular warbling sound, the result of those hand-pumped bellows.

Charles said the organ must become more than the machine it is. It must seem alive! In 1968 he proposed that the barely perceptible warble of days gone by be restored to the tracker organ, that the modern superconsistent electric blowers and wind-supply regulators not be allowed to smudge the beauty, the natural grace of the past.

Fisk's proposal was vigorously denounced by his colleagues at the time. It would take them a decade or so to see it his way.

The point is—Charles Fisk is a proud reactionary. He has devoted his life to showing us why not all we call progress is progress.

With loving hands, Charles Fisk fashions the charm of a thousand yesterdays from the same materials our ancestors used.

Charles Fisk is a purist artist who invited only peace and beauty into his world and into ours, as though purposely averting his gaze from some terrible vision—as though attempting to atone for a past unpardonable sin.

For there was a private nightmare in the life of Charles Fisk.

It happened before Stanford and before Harvard, when the slender, brown-haired boy genius in electronics was sent to Chicago to work on the top-secret Manhattan Project and then, at the age of twenty, to the laboratories of Los Alamos, New Mexico. There he had spent the remainder of World War II. And there the same hands, which now lovingly, repentantly fashion instruments of sonic glory and spiritual peace, once created instruments of terror and destruction.

It was organ builder Charles Fisk who before turning from a brilliant career in electronics and nuclear physics, helped to devise the detonators for the world's first atomic bombs!

53. The Great Manhattan Swindle

IN THE AUTUMN OF the year 1626, a politician in the city of Amsterdam wrote the following letter to the legislative assembly of the Netherlands:

> HIGH AND MIGHTY LORDS,
> Here arrived yesterday the ship . . . which on the 23rd September sailed from New Netherland . . . They report that our people there are of good cheer and live peaceably. Their wives have also borne children there. They have bought the island Manhattes (sic) from the savages for the value of sixty guilders . . .

And that is the earliest-known document relating to the local history of Manhattan Island. It also refers to something which would one day be called history's greatest real estate deal, the purchase of the island itself, for what amounted to twenty-four dollars' worth of beads and trinkets.

This much we learned in grammar school.

It was only after the English swiped Manhattan from the Dutch that it came to be known as New York. Prior to that time it was known as New Amsterdam, the governmental seat of the Dutch colony New Netherland.

Peter Minuit was the original director-general of the colony. He made all the laws, acted as judge in all legal matters. His authority was unquestionable. It was he, acting on behalf of the Dutch West India Company, who personally purchased Manhattan from the Canarsie Indians on May 6, 1626.

To put things in perspective, the island is thirteen and a

half miles long, two and a half miles wide at its widest, approximately twenty-two square miles of land.

Minuit acquired it at about a dollar a square mile.

Historians are fond of citing, for the sake of comparison, a real estate transaction which occurred some three centuries later: one square *foot* at the corner of Nassau and Wall streets for $622.29.

Your pocket calculator won't even compute that rate of appreciation. There is not enough room for the figures.

More than 391 *billion* percent.

If not fair, Peter Minuit's purchase from the Indians was legal. There was even an ornate document to seal the deal.

In the years since, the transaction has been listed among the shames of the white man. The Great Manhattan Swindle. The early European colonists, of course, rarely reimbursed the Indians at all for the lands they settled. Still, could twenty-four dollars seriously be considered reimbursement for such an enormous piece of property?

Well, this was the white man's real problem: He never gave the red man enough credit for shrewdness.

For the purchasing power of the dollar in 1626 was such that in modern equivalent, Peter Minuit actually paid many thousands of dollars for Manhattan.

And one thing more, he purchased the island from the Canarsie Indians. But the Canarsies did not live there. They were only visiting.

What I'm saying is—the Canarsie Indians sold something they never owned in the first place.

And after they ripped off the world's smartest real estate dealer, they got in their canoes and returned home.

To Brooklyn.

Now you know THE REST OF THE STORY.

54. Destiny

EVERYONE REMEMBERS THE ALAMO. And yet a surprisingly short while ago, in April of 1914, the United States once more stood at the brink of war with Mexico.

It was President Wilson's hope to spare Mexicans the military dictatorship of Victoriano Huerta. So the president, without consent of Congress, dispatched our armed forces to occupy the city of Veracruz. That was accomplished at a cost of five hundred lives.

Next it was decided that we needed a spy, someone to perform a reconnaissance operation and determine our enemy's preparedness.

Such a man was selected and sent to Veracruz. He was a captain in the U.S. Army.

Arriving May 1, he discovered no means by which our troops could be effectively deployed. Railroad cars, freight and passenger, sat empty on nearby tracks, but there were no engines to pull them. Learning that the engines had been hidden somewhere between Veracruz and Alvarado, the captain set out on a daring expedition.

He and a Mexican railroad man he had hired to accompany him began their journey by handcar. Gloomy twilight fell quickly into night. The two reached Boca del Rio but found that the railroad bridge which had spanned the Jamapa River was down. So the captain and his companion searched the riverbank, located a small boat, made the crossing.

Two stolen ponies would ride them along the tracks to another handcar. They traveled many miles more, and then, shortly after 1 A.M., five locomotives were discovered. The captain inspected them carefully, found them in need of a few minor parts but otherwise in excellent condition. Now, the hard part: He must live to tell.

On the return journey to Veracruz, the captain reached Salinas undetected. Then suddenly he and his companion were accosted by five armed men, obviously members of a marauding band. The *banditos* opened fire and gave chase. The captain and the railroad man fled, outdistancing all but two. In a hail of bullets the captain returned fire. Both pursuers went down.

At Piedra, another ambush—this time fifteen armed, mounted bandits. Another gun battle. The railroad man was shot in the shoulder, but again he and the captain escaped.

Near Laguna, still another ambush. Three mounted men thundered alongside the handcar, shooting as they rode. A shrill clanging as bullets struck the handcar, inches from the captain. And yet somehow he lost two and killed the third.

By daybreak the comrades had crossed the Jamapa River. Soon they would be in Veracruz, safely behind U.S. lines.

Recommended for the Medal of Honor, the captain was turned down—because he had followed the orders of his superiors in Washington too carefully!

He had been told that he must not confide his mission to the general in charge of U.S. occupation, for that general's own protection. And yet the awards board refused to cite the captain for bravery because he had "ignored the local commander." So instead of a medal they gave a desk job to young Captain Douglas MacArthur.

It's been said that when a man's life is destined for a special purpose, he is made invincible until that purpose is fulfilled. Might Captain MacArthur have pondered such a destiny when he returned to Veracruz that morning, wondering how he had survived the torrent of lead, then to examine his uniform?

His shirt, riddled with bullet holes.

His body, not a scratch.

Now you know THE REST OF THE STORY.

55. Darling, I Am Growing Old

> DARLING, I AM GROWING OLD,
> Silver threads among the gold,
> Shine upon my brow today,
> Life is fading fast away;
> But, my darling you will be,
> Always young and fair to me.

Their names were Hart and Hattie, and it's been said that they had one of those storybook romances.

They married in 1858 when Hart was twenty-four, a young songwriter struggling for recognition.

Hart Danks's career total is estimated at some thirteen hundred published songs, sacred and popular.

I believe you would recognize the title of only one: "Silver Threads Among the Gold."

Hart Danks was a sentimentalist. When he discovered that lyric, that poem by a Wisconsin man named Rexford, he, Hart, then thirty-eight, envisioned his own distant future.

> Darling, I am growing old,
> Silver threads among the gold . . .
> But, my darling you will be,
> Always young and fair to me . . .

Hart heard himself saying those words to his wife in the December of their lives. So he purchased the rights to the poem and began writing the now-famous melody.

It was, the historians say, a romantic gesture specifically for Hart's darling Hattie. . . .

> When your hair is silver white,
> And your cheeks no longer bright,
> With the roses of the May
> I will kiss your lips and say:
> Oh! my darling mine alone,
> You have never older grown . . .

The song was completed in 1872, was published the following year.

It was a huge hit. Sold hundreds of thousands of sheet music copies, eventually millions.

For the rest of his life Hart Danks tried to top himself, or at least to repeat that one overwhelming success of "Silver Threads."

He never did.

In thirteen hundred songs, Hart wrote virtually nothing that would be remembered beyond his own lifetime, with the exception of that wistful, sentimental forecast of the old age he had hoped to share with Hattie.

But this is THE REST OF THE STORY.

The same year "Silver Threads" was published, Hart and Hattie separated.

One year later they were divorced.

No one knows why.

It has been suggested that the workaholic in Hart submerged the sentimentalist. Or perhaps the success of "Silver Threads" simply went to Hart's head.

In any case, Hart and Hattie broke up.

Perhaps the next time you hear that song, that tribute to Hattie, that hope of comforting togetherness in old age, maybe you'll remember the chilly day in November of 1903 when Hart's sixty-nine-year-old lifeless body was discovered in a desolate Philadelphia rooming house.

His hand clutched a piece of paper on which these words were scrawled: "It is hard to die alone. . . ."

Now you know THE REST OF THE STORY.

56. The Lovely Desdemona

SOME OF THE WORLD'S best audiences are soldiers. They crave the escape of entertainment.

In September of 1845 the U.S. Fourth Infantry Regiment arrived at Corpus Christi, Texas. General Zachary Taylor's men. Three thousand of them.

In months the border brawl which history recalls as the Mexican War would be under way. For the time being, the long winter, the waiting game.

Camp followers rushed in to fill the boredom vacuum, set up gambling dens to amuse the men.

The commanders were not amused.

They appealed to Lieutenant John Magruder to provide an alternative recreation, anything to distract the men from vice.

Magruder, a society gentleman from Virginia, had just the idea. . . .

A theater!

He would instruct the enlisted men to build an eight-hundred-seat theater and the officers to paint scenery, and the soldiers would be entertained by the finest theatrical productions.

The theater was constructed. It opened January 8.

The infantrymen, seeing their commanding officers eagerly buying tickets, bought tickets also, and thus were production costs soon covered.

First, the military audiences were treated to a light comedy. Tremendous success.

Then the soldiers were offered something heavy, a tragedy, Shakespeare's *Othello*.

By now the men's theatrical taste was a bit elevated, their perception of dramatic fine points sharpened. They found something wrong, or at least something imprecise, about that Shakespearean production.

It was one of the characters. Desdemona.

The lovely Desdemona. The gentle innocent who said: "A guiltless death I die," and was smothered in her bed.

The object of jealousy and passion, the fair Desdemona rose above it all while she lived. And yet in the Corpus Christi production of 1846, she was lacking something. Desdemona was not quite right.

The talented Theodoric Porter, who played the part of Othello, was the first to come out and say it. This Desdemona was uninspiring, he declared. And so, properly to inspire the leading man, the company went in search of a new Desdemona.

They found her in New Orleans, a well-known actress named Hart. To Corpus Christi, for Zach Taylor's troops, she came, she performed, she conquered.

But this is THE REST OF THE STORY.

Before that actress joined the company, the company was comprised entirely of soldiers. Men. As in Shakespeare's time, the role of Desdemona had been performed by a man.

They had dressed a rather good-looking young officer in crinolines and given him the part, and as a fair young woman he did look smashing! Only in historical perspective is that puzzling. . . .

For the young officer's less-than-success as a dramatic actress was quickly forgiven, forgotten.

You remember instead the general and the president he became—grizzle-bearded, hard-riding, hard-drinking, cigar-chomping *Ulysses S. Grant*.

57. Getting the Message

WE GOT NO RESPECT. In the beginnings of our nation, we got no respect. At the time they called it the Second War of Independence. Every high school student knows it as the War of 1812. The problem was, we got no respect.

Europe simply did not take the United States seriously as such. England and France, for instance, engaged in their own conflict, refused to accept American neutrality. That's where the trouble really began. While France and England were slugging it out, we, as a neutral nation, were able to trade with both feuding parties. In the early years of the Anglo-French War, American shipping benefited enormously.

Then, in 1805, the British determined that no U.S. vessel would be permitted to carry goods from the colonies of France to the motherland, even with a stopover at a U.S. port.

Napoleon then countered with orders that any neutral vessel sailing into a British port, or paying British duties, or even allowing itself to be searched by a British vessel, would be subject to confiscation by the government of France. That was, of course, a French blockade of the British Isles.

Predictably, Britain counter-countered, declaring that the ports of France and its colonies and its allies were now off limits to neutral vessels, unless those vessels first docked at British ports to pay British duties on their cargoes!

And so was American trade confronted with a double blockade. To have obeyed the decree of either nation would have risked confiscation by the other! It was for that reason that the United States decided to heed—neither. Our position was that the British and French blockades violated international law.

As the months passed, the French gave us less trouble, the British gave us more. In fact, the British developed the nasty habit of stopping American ships on the high seas and impressing the American seamen into the British navy! We got no respect.

In 1811, Napoleon announced that U.S. vessels could trade wherever and with whomever they wanted, that as far as the U.S. was concerned there was no French blockade. But the British council still refused to revoke its earlier decree. England would continue to interfere with American commerce in any way she could. We got no respect.

Finally President James Madison decided it was time we got some.

June 1, 1812, he said so in a message to Congress. "We behold our seafaring citizens still the daily victims of lawless violence," he exclaimed. "We behold our vessels . . . wrested from their lawful destinations."

And Congress listened. On June 18 came the official declaration of war.

I say, on June *18*. It is most important that you remember that date.

For the history books tell us that the United States went to war with Great Britain for the second time in thirty-six years and that it was a costly war in both money and lives.

But this is THE REST OF THE STORY.

On June *16*, two days prior to our declaration of war on Britain, a motion was entered before the British council that interference with U.S. commerce was to cease.

And that motion was passed.

Yet so time-consuming was transatlantic communication in those days that we didn't find out until it was too late to back out.

We entered the War of 1812 after the reasons for that war were no more!

58. Close to His Heart

BERT WAS A SHORT-STORY WRITER.

A successful one.

He wrote for magazines mostly, about twenty short stories and five serials a year. Fiction, of course. Every imaginable topic. But one.

There was one potential short-story subject repeatedly rejected by Bert's editors.

And wouldn't you know it? It was the one subject closest to Bert's heart: dogs.

For ten years Bert had been begging magazine editors to let him write dog stories. Bert knew dogs. He had been studying them all his life, even raised them at his country home in northern New Jersey. Yet almost automatically the editors said no.

They said dog stories were outdated.

They said the public appetite was for "spicy" literature.

So at last, after a decade of objections, Bert gave up on the notion of writing about dogs.

Then came that one wonderful weekend in 1914.

One of the magazines he wrote for was the *Red Book*. Editor Ray Long often visited Bert at the writer's country home. Bert's wife would prepare home-cooked meals, and the two men would discuss story plots or simply enjoy the pastoral surroundings.

On one such weekend, author and editor were relaxing—when editor Ray Long inquired about one of Bert's dogs.

The dog seemed rather aloof, even unfriendly.

Bert explained that was just the dog's nature, trusting of master and mistress, yet coldly indifferent toward everyone else. Houseguests were always trying to win the dog over, coax him closer, draw him within petting range, and always unsuccessfully.

Ray said it was a shame. Such a handsome animal! And the subject was about to be changed.

When to everyone's astonishment the dog—that same habitually aloof dog—walked up to where magazine editor Ray Long was sitting and laid his paw and his head on Ray's knee!

Ray reacted as would you or I. He just felt all warm inside. For while such an expression of affection would have been touching from any animal, from this particular animal it was a downright tribute.

In fact, editor Ray was so moved that he later asked author Bert to write a story for the *Red Book*—a story about that very dog!

Bert had always wanted to write a dog story. For ten years he had tried to convince various magazine editors that he should. And now, after he had given up on the idea, his own pet dog cinched the deal.

The story appeared in the *Red Book* in January of 1915, the first of many stories to follow, and all about Bert's pet. Even the name remained unchanged.

The name of Bert's independent canine companion who just once snuggled up to a stranger, a magazine editor, and became immortal.

The personal pet of Bert. Albert Payson Terhune.

He became the most popular writer of animal stories since Kipling by sharing with us the adventures of an animal particularly close to his heart, a handsome collie called "Lad."

Lad, who begat Lassie.

Now you know THE REST OF THE STORY.

59. The Deadly Honeymoon

IT WAS THE DAY after the wedding, and the happy couple had not yet emerged from the bridal chamber.

The wedding celebration had gone long into the night, so the bride and groom were not really expected to be stirring until afternoon.

I'm not sure what it was that aroused the suspicion of friends. I do not know why, but after a while they grew concerned, went to the door of the bridal chamber, and began shouting the groom's name.

No answer.

They shouted again. Again, silence.

So the groom's comrades broke down the door. And once inside, they beheld a gruesome sight.

The lovely young bride was kneeling at the bedside, weeping bitterly.

The groom lay on the bed.

Dead.

The groom had died on his own wedding night. Murder?

Let's consider the evidence.

The bride, an exceptionally pretty German girl, was not the groom's first wife. According to her, she had awakened to discover the husband was dead.

He had had a great deal to drink the night before.

That was all she knew.

Indeed, there were no marks on the groom's body, no apparent wounds that might have led to his death.

Obviously the grieving bride was telling the truth. Anyway, she had no motive to kill her husband.

But if she did not kill him, what did?

And then someone remembered—the nosebleeds.

The groom had suffered from chronic epistaxis, repeated hemorrhaging of the nasal capillaries.

A brief examination told THE REST OF THE STORY.

The groom had fallen into a drunken stupor and then a deep sleep.

He was flat on his back when his nose began to bleed.

Within minutes he had suffocated, drowned in his own blood.

Case closed.

History offers other versions of the incident you have just relived, even invents conceivable motives for the bride to have stabbed her groom in the night. Those other versions, however, are based on rumors which arose later.

It would be of no interest to us today, more than fifteen hundred years after the fact, except for the groom's impact on his own era.

He had a great many enemies. So it was not unreasonable initially to suspect his young bride Ildico of murder.

Yet as far as we know, the groom's demise occurred just as you've learned: too much booze and a nosebleed.

Odd end for a man once called "the Scourge of God," whose name struck terror throughout the Western world.

Having survived a lifetime of brutal battles, he was at last done in by his own honeymoon.

The reputedly "indestructible" Attila the Hun partied himself to death!

60. Alan's Unabridged

NOW, IT'S ANYTHING GOES. Pornography comes directly into your living room through a cable.

Yet once upon a time, you would have had to leave the country to see a pornographic movie or to buy a sexually explicit publication.

When Alan was living in Europe, he bought and read a dirty book. It was widely available there, and much of the material raised the young American journalist's eyebrows.

When Alan returned home, he brought the book with him.

And then he noticed that same book was on sale here in the United States.

Almost the same book.

A censored version.

Journalist Alan did not believe in censorship. He felt it was the American public's right to read even the most unsavory literature.

In this case a Boston publisher, the Houghton Mifflin Company, was printing a laundered version of this dirty European book, three dollars a copy.

Alan was outraged. He brought the matter to the attention of New York newspaperman Amster Spiro.

Both men agreed that there was no justification for the censorship. Alan proposed that they publish their own version of the book in the United States—that is, the original version translated into English. While the fumigated Houghton Mifflin edition was selling for three dollars, Alan and his

friend could make their no-holds-barred edition available for
ten cents a copy!

Alan spent a week at his friend's home in Connecticut,
working painstakingly on the original translation. After his
eighth eighteen-hour day, it was finished.

Alan's edition was published quickly. In days the book was
offered at booksellers and magazine stands nationwide. A half-
million copies were sold during its first ten days on the racks.

Then, the predictable legal action. The courts ruled that
Alan's publication was to be taken out of the stores and off the
stands.

And it was.

But by then, Alan had made his point: The worst thing you
can do to a dirty book—is try to clean it up.

Californians know and respect the man that young journalist became, U.S. Senator Alan Cranston.

Before you evaluate what he did back in 1938, you should
know something about the litigation that got his publication
pulled off the shelves.

The *author* of the original book had sued Alan for violation
of copyright. It had been the author's *intention* to publish a
watered-down version of his work in the United States, because he did not want Americans to know THE REST OF THE
STORY.

Young Alan Cranston and fellow publisher Amster Spiro
wanted us to recognize the long-range plans of author Adolf
Hitler: German military expansion and the liquidation of the
Jews. So they, Cranston and Spiro, published the unlaun-
dered version of the world's dirtiest book, *Mein Kampf.*

61. The Model Son

ANNA WAS A STRICT PARENT, also a loving one. Her boy Bill was the model son.

As a child he was positive, robust, obedient, intelligent. Mother Anna often remarked what a fine doctor her Bill would make, so Bill grew determined that his mother's wish come true.

When he went to study medicine in Philadelphia, Anna went with him, kept house for him so he could concentrate on his studies.

During the War Between the States Bill joined the Confederate Army as a military surgeon. He was to spend most of the war in Richmond. And do you know that his mother Anna actually ran the blockade from north to south, just to visit her son Bill?

Shortly thereafter, she traveled to London where the rest of the family was gathered. Bill said, "Don't worry, I'll join you there soon."

I believe the months that followed comprised Bill's longest separation ever from his mother.

Early in 1865, he was assigned to carry dispatches through the lines to New York, and from there on to England. Those were special Confederate communications to the British government.

Anyway, the war was over in April. Anna and Bill were already reunited in London. Bill decided they would stay there.

Bill was not authorized to practice medicine in England

right away, but soon he acquired the necessary credentials and specialized in respiratory diseases.

In time he became a much respected expert in that field, really one of the finest physicians in London.

And who was with him through it all to share in his successes? His proud mother, Anna.

The only specter looming over this otherwise pleasant horizon was the weather. London's fog and damp did not agree with Anna. Each winter she became ill. She barely survived the winter of 1875. But, of course, her boy Bill was there to nurse her back to health.

You see now why we've called him the model son. All through his life he was very good to his mom. But this is THE REST OF THE STORY.

Bill had a brother, a two-years-older brother named Jim.

In most ways what one was, the other was not.

You'll remember that when Bill was a youngster he was robust and obedient. Jim was frail and by no means as well behaved as Bill.

Jim was destined to be considerably less than the model son.

Jim was a problem in school.

Jim knew well that his mother wanted him to become a clergyman, but he rebelled, went his own way.

Jim allowed years to pass without even visiting his mother.

During the last years of Anna's life, Jim neglected her, saying he could not bear the sight of illness. It was only after she died that Jim realized he might have been kinder, might at least have written his mother more often.

His remorse had come too late.

Brother Bill had been the "good boy," the respectable physician who had adored and obeyed his mother, who had given her his time and his care.

It was brother Jim who virtually ignored her, except once when he immortalized her with a single painting.

You might say this has been the story of Anna, a mother with a model son and another not so model one.

But really, this has been the story of a man history forgot, good guy Dr. William Whistler, the brother of rebellious artist James.

What I'm saying is—you would recognize *Whistler's Mother* anywhere. Now you also have met Whistler's *brother*.

62. Danny Went West

IN 1816 THERE WAS NO Kansas City, Missouri. There was in that vicinity, however, a small military outpost, a fort on the fringe of what was then our American frontier, Fort Osage.

Late in the year that outpost was visited by a fellow named Danny. He was dressed in crude clothing, the kind worn by indigent hunters. Would the officers at the fort mind putting him up for a while? No, he was told, they would not mind.

So Danny remained at Fort Osage for two weeks, during which the soldiers learned THE REST OF THE STORY.

For years Danny had been hearing wonderful stories about the western wilderness. He had been told about the fabulous lakes and rivers, of the grand mountains which lay beyond. Danny wanted to explore them. He wanted to taste the fresh water and savor the sweet air and see the crests of the Rockies surge upward into a shimmering blue sky.

The men at Fort Osage appreciated Danny's youthful enthusiasm. Decades before Horace Greeley would proclaim, "Go West, young man, and grow up with the country," Danny was determined to go West.

Still, the soldiers wondered if Danny knew what he was getting into. A half-dozen years before, in 1810, mountain man John Colter had returned from that beckoning wilderness, the area which now so intrigued Danny, and he, Colter, had just barely emerged with his life. After the Blackfoot Indians had captured and almost killed him, the weather and the wilderness itself had nearly finished him off.

Wouldn't Danny be just as happy back in the Missouri

Territory, the soldiers wondered? There was still much hunting and exploring to be done in those virgin forests, enough excitement to satisfy any eager adventurer.

No, Danny protested, Missouri was getting too crowded, too civilized. He reckoned he'd be moving on.

And he did.

He left Fort Osage, headed north up the Missouri River, then west on the Platte River across what is now the state of Nebraska.

Danny followed the Platte all the way to the Rocky Mountains.

When he ran out of river, he traveled overland. He crossed what is now Wyoming, northwest into Yellowstone country.

Danny had plunged almost a thousand miles into a land about which white men were only beginning to dream. A rugged, dangerous journey. Threatened by Indians, he eluded them. Besieged by bitter weather, he survived.

After a season exploring that sometimes perilous, always awesome wilderness wonderland, Danny returned to the Missouri Territory to tell what he had seen.

In one respect, his trek was unremarkable. For if anyone should have found his way all that way and back, he should have. You see, Danny was known as Kentucky's original settler, a trailblazer with no rival, Colonel Daniel Boone.

And one thing more.

When Daniel Boone visited Fort Osage in 1816 before embarking on his journey of almost a thousand miles, westward on the Platte River, to the Rockies, to the Yellowstone, and almost a thousand miles back—before he had even *begun* that journey he, Boone, was eighty-two years old!

63. *The Doll in the Attic*

ON JOHN'S DESK AT WORK there was always a doll. A child's doll carefully, lovingly propped in its own special corner, watching over the day's business.

The doll never stayed in the office overnight. John brought her each morning, placed her in that special corner of his desk where she could see everything that went on, and then took her home each evening.

No one at work ever asked John about the doll.

No one had to.

Everyone who knew John knew THE REST OF THE STORY.

It was a snowy December day shortly before Christmas 1914 when eight-year-old Marcella Gruelle decided to visit her daddy.

Daddy, John Gruelle, was a political cartoonist for the *Indianapolis Star*. Little Marcella trudged all the way there through the swirling white from their home, many blocks away.

She was not alone.

She had brought with her—a doll.

Daddy kissed the snowflakes from Marcell's long lashes and gave her a big bear hug. It was wonderful that she had come to see him, he said. But Daddy was working on something called a deadline. He would have to get all of his work done soon, or the man who had hired Daddy would be very upset.

Marcella understood. But there was just one thing. The little girl had been playing in the attic. And she had found this doll. The doll was sad, she told her daddy, because it had no face. Wasn't there any way Daddy could make the doll happy again?

John Gruelle lifted the doll from his daughter's arms, smiling. Indeed, it had no eyes, no nose, no mouth—no face at all. But John recognized the tattered doll as having belonged to his mother, once upon a distant time.

John's gaze returned to little Marcella, and again he smiled. Very well, the doll would be given a face. Hastily with his pen the cartoonist sketched in the basic features, making them happy, of course. And Marcella, happy also, returned home.

Mommy mended and restuffed the dolly, even sewed a little red heart on its chest with the words "I love you" written inside.

When one day Marcella became ill and had to stay in bed, the little dolly stayed with her, constantly comforting. Daddy even made up marvelous adventure stories about the doll to amuse Marcella and to encourage her to get well. But the little girl seemed to grow increasingly frail, spending more and more time in bed. A chronic illness, the doctor said, from which Marcella would never recover.

And she did not.

She died one day in 1916—with the floppy cloth dolly clutched in her arms.

You understand now about the doll on John's desk, why he brought it to work with him each morning and took it home with him each night.

That was Marcella's doll.

The political cartoons of John Gruelle are mostly forgotten.

But the world will always remember his daughter's doll. Because not long after Marcella's death, John began writing down the stories he had once told his little girl. And those dozens of illustrated stories he shared with the rest of us, in memory of the dolly's mistress, and in memory of the long-ago Christmastime when a daddy and his little girl gave a tattered cloth doll a face.

And a name.

Raggedy Ann.

64. They Knew Too Much

WHEN THE SAILING SHIP *Discovery* departed London, April 17, 1610, there were twenty-four men aboard.

Eighteen months later, almost to the day, the *Discovery* returned to London—*minus* sixteen men!

The eight men remaining were mutineers. Their story is THE REST OF THE STORY.

By midsummer 1610 the crew was demoralized, frightened, anxious to turn the ship around and head for home. The bleak, fog-cradled coastline looming before them made the men even more fearful.

The captain, however, was eager to press onward. Madness, the crew began calling it. Especially after one dreadful winter had passed.

In June of 1611, some of the crew members met secretly to discuss their predicament. Rationalizing that their own survival was at stake, they plotted a meeting.

The night of the twenty-third, they grabbed the captain and those loyal to him and put them all in a small boat. The deposed captain, his son, and six officers were given nothing to eat, nothing to drink, nothing to wear—nothing. They were simply cast adrift, sentenced to a certain death in the icy waters.

The mutineers were not in much better shape. Some were killed by natives they encountered on the way home; others starved to death. As you've already learned, eight men survived to guide their vessel into the mouth of the Thames and into port at London.

Now, the British knew all about mutiny. Yet I'm not sure if what happened next had ever happened before or would ever happen again.

The owners of the sailing ship *Discovery* interrogated the surviving mutineers immediately upon their arrival. When the interrogation was over, it was agreed unanimously that the survivors should now be hanged.

But wait!—the owners made no such recommendation to the High Court of Admiralty. In fact, a whole year had passed before the High Court even questioned one of the survivors!

Eventually, four of the mutineers were tried. By eventually, I mean seven full *years* after the mutiny had taken place. Those four who were tried were promptly acquitted!

The history books call it a "shocking miscarriage of justice"—and that's not all.

One of the surviving mutineers had gone on to serve as a ship's surgeon, and another as a bo'sun's mate, and still another mutineer officially became *captain* of the *Discovery*, the very ship on which he had committed mutiny!

A ship's captain, his son, and six officers were as much as murdered, yet the British authorities dared not exterminate the men responsible.

Those men, those eight mutineers, knew too much. They were too valuable to hang!

For they had sailed hitherto uncharted waters, and only they knew the way back.

Their claim was that they had discovered the Northwest Passage.

They had not.

But that claim saved their skins.

What they *had* discovered and described as a great "sea to the westward" was subsequently named for the captain against whom that historic mutiny was committed, the body of water in which Captain Henry Hudson was cast adrift and from which he was never heard again—Canada's vast *Hudson Bay*.

65. A Love Story

SARAH WAS A SLENDER, tender young lady of eighteen with hazel eyes and luxuriant, wavy brown hair. She was the daughter of a colonel in the United States Army, stationed at Prairie du Chien, Wisconsin.

It was during the sunny August of 1832 that Sarah fell in love. Her beau, a twenty-four-year-old lieutenant serving under her father. He was a tall, handsome, idealistic young man named Jeff.

Right from the beginning Sarah's daddy, the colonel, disapproved.

Nothing personal, he said. He just didn't want his daughter "marrying into the army." He'd seen enough of the sacrifices made by army wives, including his own.

At least, that is what he said. But the more Sarah's daddy insisted that he had "no personal objections" to the young lieutenant, the more obvious it became that he really did.

We're not sure what those objections were. Some say they were based on a petty disagreement between the two. Others hint it was a matter of some minor misconduct on the lieutenant's behalf.

In any event, the colonel's antipathy only intensified, especially after Sarah and Jeff announced their engagement. In fact, Daddy became so furious that he absolutely forbade the young lieutenant ever to enter his home again!

Of course, the colonel's home was also Sarah's home, which presented the young lovers with a rather serious obstacle.

Jeff got angry—so angry that he actually considered challenging the father of his betrothed, a superior officer, to a duel! Friends talked him out of it, promised to help Jeff arrange surreptitious meetings with Sarah. They did, and the beleaguered romance survived.

It survived the vigilance of Sarah's daddy.

It survived Jeff's promotion to first lieutenant and his subsequent transfer from Prairie du Chien to a fort in the Southwest.

And in June of 1835, shortly after Jeff had resigned his army commission, Sarah went to visit an aunt in Beechland, Kentucky—ostensibly for a "visit"—and married Jeff instead.

After the shock over his daughter's impetuous decision had worn off, the colonel found something else to worry about.

He learned that the newlyweds would be honeymooning in the Deep South, that in fact they planned to live on a southern plantation—and "fever season" was approaching.

On August 11, Sarah wrote to her mother with assurances that she was well and that the southern climate was "quite healthy."

Days later, in West Feliciana Parish, Louisiana, both Sarah and Jeff contracted malaria.

On the fifteenth of September, less than three months after their wedding day, Jeff rose unsteadily from his own sickbed, staggered into the room where Sarah lay—just in time to take her in his arms as the bright hazel eyes that had captured his heart closed forever.

Many months passed before young Jeff was physically well again. His spirit was not so easily healed. Eight bitter years following the death of his bride were spent in total seclusion.

Subsequently, and by chance, Jeff met Sarah's father aboard a riverboat on the Mississippi. The tragedy they shared brought peace between them. Thereafter, both men seemed to be fired with inexorable ambition.

Sarah's daddy, the colonel, who by then had become a

general, eventually became President of the United States, Zachary Taylor.

And young Jeff, who had also walked through the fire, also emerged heat-tempered. As some have said, "intellectually reborn."

For he, put to the test of living without Sarah, set out upon his own path of immortality accompanied by her memory, the gentle ghost of once upon a springtime.

He became a U.S. congressman, a colonel of volunteers, a U.S. senator, a secretary of war—and ultimately President of the Confederacy, Jefferson Davis.

Now you know THE REST OF THE STORY.

66. They Found Us First

THE FIRST SPANISH EXPLORERS reached the New World in 1492. The first English, five years later. The first French, twenty-seven years after that.

All three historic voyages had something remarkable in common.

In elementary school you were taught that "Columbus discovered America in 1492," and that he was trying to prove the world was round. In fact, the Norsemen had already discovered America in the 11th century, and Columbus did not actually reach an American continent until 1498. The roundness of the world was never in question for him. What Christopher was trying to do was find a shortcut to the Indies.

He had been corresponding with a gentleman in Florence who believed that Japan was only three thousand nautical miles west of Lisbon, Portugal. The prospect of proving this was irresistible to Columbus.

There were ninety men on that first voyage in 1492.

The feeling of futility was such that on October 10, all agreed to sail three more days and then return home if no land were found. San Salvador was sighted in the moonlit early morning of October 12.

Columbus insisted San Salvador was an island not far from Japan or China, one of the Indies group. Almost three decades would pass before Columbus was proved wrong. Of course, we still call the New World natives he discovered—Indians.

When Chris returned from his first voyage, all of Europe was tantalized.

The English vessel *Matthew* sailed westward from Bristol in 1497. Her captain was John Cabot. Certain that Columbus had reached the East Indies, Cabot grew convinced that he could discover an even shorter route to the north.

There were eighteen men in Cabot's crew.

In thirty-five days he made land. Big land. Probably Maine or southern Nova Scotia. He went ashore, claimed the continent for England. There was no doubt in Cabot's mind: He had reached Asia.

Returning to England in August, he was hailed as "the great admiral." The king rewarded him with a handsome lump sum and an annual pension.

The French would not seek the New World until 1524. That's when Jean Verrazano set sail at the behest of King Francis I.

Maps being what they were it is difficult to be certain, but historians generally agree that Verrazano explored the North American coast from Cape Fear to Cape Breton. He discovered New York Harbor and Narragansett Bay. He explored the shores of New England. He may even have touched land at what is now North Carolina.

Columbus, Cabot, Varrazano. The first Spanish exploration, the first English exploration, the first French exploration of the New World.

And all three historic voyages had something remarkable in common: the nationality of their captains.

"Spanish" Captain Christopher Columbus. Real name: Cristoforo Columbo.

"English" Captain John Cabot. Real name: Giovanni Caboto.

"French" Captain Jean Verrazano. Real name: Giovanni da Verrazano.

To command their first New World explorations, the

Spanish and the English and the French governments chose sea captains born in *Italy*.

And so busy were the Italians sailing for other nations that not one Italian vessel ever explored the New World!

Now you know THE REST OF THE STORY.

67. The Boy Who Outshot Annie Oakley

IN MAY OF 1883, Buffalo Bill and his *Wild West Show* came to Chicago. The first Sunday, some forty thousand city dwellers converged on the tents in the park, eager to witness Bill Cody's re-creation of his adventures on the American frontier.

It was the sort of event to be witnessed through the eyes of a young boy, and so we shall.

He was barely fourteen, had been saving admission money for months in anticipation of Buffalo Bill's Chicago appearances. On weekdays, while the show was in town, he played hooky from school to see his heroes perform—names now forgot, such as Buck Taylor and Johnnie Baker and David Payne, and one name remembered to this day: Annie Oakley.

The youngster was thrilled by Annie Oakley's demonstrations of marksmanship

One afternoon Buffalo Bill strode before his audience and announced that a free pass would be awarded anyone who could outshoot sure-shot Annie.

Recalled are only the essentials of what happened next: The fourteen-year-old boy you've just met stepped from the crowd, challenged Annie Oakley to target shooting, and won the free pass.

That is all we know for sure.

No one remembers the kind of targets that were used, nor how a youngster unfamiliar with firearms could possibly have beaten Annie Oakley in a marksmanship contest.

On the other hand, and contrary to what might be suspected in this instance, it is unlikely that the shooting match was rigged. And I'll tell you why.

Buffalo Bill Cody was apparently sufficiently impressed by the youngster's skill to invite him to join the traveling *Wild West Show*.

Without telling his parents, the boy accepted. His father, the straitlaced founder and president of the Chicago Musical College, would never have given his permission anyway.

So the boy decided he would wait until the *Wild West Show* was leaving town, and he, quietly, would leave with it.

As it turned out, his evaluation of his father's sentiments was correct. But he had underestimated Dad's persistence in tracking him down.

It was, they say, at the next stop on the traveling show's tour, in a small town near Chicago, that Dad found his son performing in a buckskin jacket with a pair of six-guns strapped to his sides.

The boy's *last* performance, his father declared.

He would come home and go back to school and learn to become a college administrator. And, above all, he would forget about show business!

But it was too late to forget about show business. The boy had heard just enough applause to be hooked forever.

In time he would emulate Buffalo Bill, at least to the point of producing his own shows.

For the youngster who played hooky in order to see Bill Cody in person, the fourteen-year-old boy who had to outshoot Annie Oakley to get his first break in show business, would one day be named among the greatest theatrical producers of all time.

Florenz Ziegfeld.

Now you know THE REST OF THE STORY.

68. President Grant's Watergate

As a general, Ulysses S. Grant was spared a "Waterloo."
And yet as president, he almost met his "Watergate."

The Grant administration was widely believed, especially
in Democratic circles, to have been a corrupt one. By the
spring of 1876, "Get-Grant" fever had spilled from the Hill
into the heartland. But congressional investigators needed
something substantial with which to nail the president. They
would begin with grand-scale graft in the War Department.
They would get *to* Grant *through* his suspect secretary of war,
William Belknap.

Under Belknap, soldiers at army posts could no longer
purchase nonmilitary supplies from whomever they wished.
Beginning June 1870, they could make such purchases only
from merchants chosen and licensed by the War Department.
Furthermore, rumor had it, those army-post merchants,
called "sutlers," were paying up to four-fifths of their annual
income to War Department officials. Some said, to Secretary
Belknap himself!

It would take more than hearsay to expose Belknap,
however.

One man came forward.

He was a soldier named George from Fort Abraham Lincoln in the Dakota Territory.

He testified before a number of congressional committees.
Yes, he had met the secretary of war when he visited Fort
Lincoln. Yes, he believed Belknap was a crook. Then he,
George, produced certain documents to support his con-

tention. He even linked Orvil Grant, the president's own brother, to Belknap's alleged indiscretions.

Before the congressional investigation was over, William Belknap resigned as secretary of war. The administration was toppling, critics said.

But President Grant weathered his "Watergate." At least, he was destined to complete this, his second term. No thanks to George.

Grant would never forget that.

In fact, the president grew determined to punish George for trying to ruin him politically, and it is easy for a commander-in-chief to punish a soldier. The choice assignments the soldier expects are one day no longer there.

George tried desperately to get back into President Grant's good graces. He visited the White House personally, sat waiting for hours before being told that the president did not want to see him.

George realized he would have to do something spectacular in order to redeem himself.

And so he set out to do something spectacular.

And he failed.

Yet he failed so spectacularly that each generation since has remembered him for it.

George, General George Armstrong Custer, was President Grant's John Dean.

But Grant survived his political scandal.

And Custer, attempting to regain the favor of the man he had sought to disgrace, planned a daring, reckless raid against the Sioux and Cheyenne, and rode to his death—at Little Big Horn.

All your life you've heard of Custer's last stand.

Now you know THE REST OF THE STORY.

69. The Survivor of Little Big Horn

OUR NATION'S CENTENNIAL CELEBRATION on July 4, 1876, was less enthusiastic than it might have been. The event was marred by something that had happened only nine days before in southern Montana: General George Custer had led his Seventh Cavalry in its final, fatal foray.

History relates that three thousand Sioux and Cheyenne were waiting for them by the Little Big Horn River, and that never before nor since have white soldiers been so decisively defeated by red ones.

The Indians' victory, however, was not so complete as we may have been led to believe. . . .

For one member of Custer's forces did survive.

Many history books boldly state that Custer and all of those under his immediate command were annihilated.

But one did not die. And his story is THE REST OF THE STORY.

A relief column of soldiers arrived too late at Little Big Horn. One can hardly imagine their horror.

The battlefield was strewn with hundreds of stripped, mulilated bodies. Violence in repose. Deafening silence.

Then one of the bodies moved.

Amidst all that carnage, a flicker of life.

One of the soldiers rushed over to assist the survivor. There were bullet and arrow wounds in his body and neck. Twelve wounds in all.

Lieutenant Henry Nowland, who immediately recognized him, ordered first aid. For the moment, all they could do was to stop the bleeding. The long fight for his life had only begun.

First, could he be moved safely? It was a chance that had to be taken.

Fifteen miles away, at the mouth of the Little Big Horn River, a steamboat was waiting to evacuate any casualties. The rescuing troopers would hurry their survivor to the vessel as quickly as possible.

Once on board, his welfare became the foremost concern of the entire crew. They broke a speed record steaming downstream to Fort Bismark; the trip took fifty-one hours.

From there, the survivor of the Battle of Little Big Horn was transported to Fort Abraham Lincoln, headquarters of the Seventh Cavalry.

It would take him almost a year to recover fully, during which time he became somewhat of a celebrity.

He was considered a hero, as though there were something heroic in having lived through Custer's last stand. Lucky is what he was, that for all the bullet and arrow wounds no vital organ was irreparably damaged.

His lifetime fringe-benefit-laced pension was unparalleled in the U.S. armed forces. And while his presence was continually requested at military ceremonies, that was the limit of his responsibility to the United States Army.

When finally he did die of natural causes in November of 1891, there would be no hero's funeral. Instead, the sole survivor among Custer's forces—the lone veteran of Little Big Horn—was stuffed and mounted and put on display in the Museum of Kansas University.

The survivor lived, but not "to tell."

He was a light bay cavalry horse named Comanche.

70. Yesler Way

WHAT IS NOW the city of Seattle, Washington, was in 1853 no more than a few staked claims in the woods. That was the year Henry Yesler arrived.

Henry said, "What this land needs is a sawmill!" And he proposed to build one at the bottom of a hill, right on the waterfront.

Of course, he would need a log run, a channel cut through the woods by which timber could be transported from the hilltop to the mill. Two local pioneers, Doc Maynard and Carson Boren, offered the dividing line of their properties.

Henry was in business.

He built his house and his steam-powered sawmill by the water's edge at the bottom of the hill, and he cut an access route from the mill to the hilltop, right on his neighbors' property line.

It was a steep incline. That made log transportation from top to bottom much easier. Henry actually smeared grease on the pathway, so the logs almost slid by themselves!

Fifteen years later . . .

Near Yesler's Mill, toward the foot of the hill, there were more homes. Doc Maynard lived in one, a blacksmith in another. Seattle was still very much a pioneer town, although there were signs of the civilized prosperity which was just around the corner.

In a few years more, the woods themselves would be history. The homes would be replaced by places of business. Henry Yesler's log run from the hilltop to the harbor would become a street, a central avenue in the downtown Seattle business district.

No one remembers precisely when Henry stopped using it as a log slide. About 1870, I think.

Thereafter it became Mill Street, and then Yesler Way in honor of town miller Henry Yesler, who contributed so much to the city's economy.

Lumber remained Seattle's principal source of income. San Francisco, several hundred miles to the south, kept burning down. And they kept rebuilding with wood from Seattle.

In 1896, gold was discovered in the Klondike. The Alaskan gold rush was on.

Prospectors swarmed into the Northwest. Money poured into Seattle. Yesler Way, once a slide for mill-bound logs, bustled as never before.

There had always been something a little risqué about Yesler Way. Even back in the early 1860s, when the logs were still descending the hill on their bellies, there was a boarding-house near the bottom with a streetside sign: "Madame Damnable." Seattle's turn-of-the-century gold wealth added glitter to the slightly naughty, bawdy backdrop.

Problem was, Seattle overbuilt in its prosperity delirium. When the bottom dropped out of the economy a decade later, when the depression swept the city, it left a lot of empty buildings and a lot of broken dreams on Yesler Way.

Seattle had been all dressed up, and now, suddenly, there was no place to go. Yesler Way reflected the desolation as no other street in the city. The down-and-outers slept in doorways there, shuffled the unswept sidewalks beneath signs that read "condemned."

The old avenue down the hill that fell from glitter to the gutter never quite got on her feet again. And she is still haunted by forgotten men who can't forget her real name.

For the Yesler Way of yesterday was Mill Street, named because it led to Henry Yesler's mill. Before that, it was named something else, in reference to the sliding logs that comprised its original traffic.

Today, it is Yesler Way—just another boulevard of broken dreams.

Yet way back when, in the pioneer days, that downhill log-run pathway had a name by which a thousand slum streets in a thousand cities would someday be called.

Yesler Way, the greased path down which the logs once skidded on their way to Yesler's Mill, was our nation's first, was the original—"Skid Road."

Now you know THE REST OF THE STORY.

71. A Slip of the Tongue

IN THE DAYS OF World War I, long before James Bond was even a matter of fiction, Bill was a real-life secret agent for British Intelligence.

His missions as such took him to Switzerland, France, Italy, America, the South Pacific—even to Russia.

In his last years, Bill retired to the Villa Mauresque on the French Riviera. It was there and then that he told his nephew THE REST OF THE STORY.

Bill was never in his life a stranger to foreign affairs. As a boy he had watched his father perform in the capacity of legal attaché to the British Embassy in Paris. Independent of this, Bill was bright, perceptive, well educated, and loyal to his beloved England.

In these ways and more, he was ideally suited to the tasks and responsibilities of a secret agent.

British Intelligence, having carefully considered his qualifications, recruited Bill from the medical corps shortly after the outbreak of World War I. Subsequently, the department entrusted him with many of its most intricate and strategically significant assignments.

Toward the end of his life, Bill lived elegantly on the French Riviera. His nephew visited him there at the Villa Mauresque, sharing with his distinguished uncle the warm breezes and the many memories.

What you are about to read we have learned from the meticulously recorded conversations between Bill and his nephew. Bill said . .

"In 1917 I was sent to Russia on a secret mission. I'd been in the secret service for some time. . . . I was given a vast sum of money by the American and the British governments. And I was sent to Petrograd . . . because they thought that I could stop the Bolshevik Revolution. With the money they'd given me . . . I was supposed to help the Mensheviks buy arms and finance newspapers so as to keep Russia in the war and to prevent the Bolsheviks from seizing power. . . ."

Bill felt personally responsible for the triumph of the Bolsheviks in Russia. "I feel a deep sense of failure, complete and utter failure," he said. He blamed, of all things, a speech impediment—his lifelong stutter! Again, in Bill's own words . . .

"One morning in the autumn Kerensky sent for me and gave me a message for [British Prime Minister] Lloyd George. It was so secret that he wouldn't put it in writing. But when I got back to London I wrote the message down because I knew that when I came to tell it to the Prime Minister I'd begin to stammer. Lloyd George was in a hurry when I met him, so I just handed him what I'd written out. And he only glanced at the note. If I'd read the memo aloud to him it might have made all the difference. And perhaps the world today might be a very different place."

No one knows, for Bill never told, just what that top-secret message was. Although it is difficult to imagine a single communiqué of such significance, it is interesting to conjecture that the Communists came to power in Russia—by a slip of the tongue.

Also, we are led to believe that Bill's speech impediment cost British Intelligence on more than that one occasion. He said: "You can have no idea what a disadvantage my stammer was to me when I was a secret agent. . . . I can't imagine why they ever chose me. . . . I was the wrong man for the job. . . . I made a hash of the whole business."

Of course, aside from his acquaintance with foreign affairs, his intelligence, his superior education, his loyalty, Bill's foremost qualification for spy work was that he possessed the perfect "cover."

For Bill, the British agent the whole free world was counting on, the man who just may have stuttered the Soviet Union into existence, was England's immortal author, William Somerset Maugham.

Now you know THE REST OF THE STORY.

72. Olga

FRED KROGG IS A Springfield, Ohio, dentist. His best friend is a black-and-tan part-collie part-German shepherd dog named Olga.

The two have been inseparable since Olga was a puppy. She accompanied her master through eight years of college, even won a dog show at the University of Dayton for her clever tricks. She is thirteen now.

It was a particularly warm, sunny Saturday afternoon in March of 1981 when Fred decided to wash his car. As always, Olga was not far away, was lying in the backyard near the driveway, listening to the hum of the vacuum Fred was using to clean his car's interior. The gentle drone seemed to be lulling Olga to sleep.

Then suddenly she jumped up. Her quick movement startled Fred, especially considering the dog's age. It had been years since Fred had seen her as lively.

She was running toward the next-door neighbor's driveway, barking insistently.

Fred followed.

The neighbor had also been washing his car, or so it seemed. For Fred discovered him sprawled on the driveway in front of his garage, motionless. Olga was there with him, licking his face.

The neighbor, Jack Werber, was gray-skinned and cold to the touch, was not breathing. Fred felt for a pulse. There was none. Jack was dead.

But dead is not nearly as dead as it was in the days before cardiopulmonary resuscitation, and so Fred administered CPR.

Mouth-to-mouth. Impacts to the chest.

Minutes, nothing.

Finally, after an interminable while, fitful, shallow breathing. To Fred's great relief, neighbor Jack was returning from the brink.

As her master pulled away, Olga, who had been close by all the time, began licking Jack's face again. Fred ran into the house, dialed 911. And when the Springfield emergency squad arrived five minutes later, they found Olga, still licking the face of her stricken neighbor.

The medics worked feverishly over Jack for several minutes, then hurried him to the hospital.

After examining Jack thoroughly, the doctors recommended that open-heart surgery be performed as soon as possible. It was. A quadruple bypass.

Jack recovered remarkably quickly. He spent only two weeks in the hospital. And the first thing he did when he got out was to buy a nice, thick, juicy steak—for Olga.

Her heroism has been the talk of the neighborhood ever since. Indeed, had Olga not jumped up and run to Jack when she did, had the dog not alerted her master to the peril of the man next door, that man surely would have died.

But Jack Werber of Springfield, Ohio, is alive today because a twelve-year-old mutt named Olga somehow knew that he was in trouble even though she, the dog, was recuperating from her own surgery the week before, surgery attempting to halt the disease that will one day take her life.

Olga had jumped up and had run to the side of the stricken neighbor. She had *run*, which she had not done in years. Because for the past three years, Olga had been irreversibly, totally blind!

Now you know THE REST OF THE STORY.

73. The Peach-Fuzz Physician

WALLY WAS A DOCTOR. Twenty-two years old. Private practice. And he was about to quit.

For in 1874, folks were disinclined to trust young physicians. Beards were advisable for that reason. A full-bearded doctor inspired confidence in his patients.

Wally sported no such dignified whiskers. He tried but simply could not grow them. Describing the disadvantages of a youthful appearance, he once wrote: "It is a remarkable fact that a man's success during the first decade depends more upon his beard than upon his brains."

And so it was that beardless Wally decided to abandon his private practice.

Wally was born in Gloucester County, Virginia, the son of a Methodist minister.

The boy was educated in private schools and was noted for his extraordinary brilliance. At fifteen he was prepared to enter the University of Virginia, where he spent one year on academics and the second year studying medicine. He received his first M.D. at age seventeen.

It took him only one more year to earn his second M.D., that from the Bellevue Hospital Medical College.

Wally interned at Kings County Hospital in Brooklyn, New York, then served on the Brooklyn board of health and the New York City board of health.

At the same time, he attempted to establish a private practice.

For years he tried.

At last the young doctor with no patients and no patience gave up.

There he was, a medical genius, the University of Virginia's youngest-ever M.D., and now at the tender age of twenty-two he was turning his back on private practice.

Actually, there were many reasons behind his decision.

One, a successful general practice in those days depended largely on social connections and personal wealth. Had Wally been wealthy, he probably would have studied the classics in college. He was much more interested in Latin and Greek and literature and philosophy than he was in the natural sciences. But at that time it was less expensive to be trained in medicine.

Another reason Wally was throwing in the towel had to do with a young lady named Emilie Lawrence. Wally wanted to marry Emilie. Unless he could be assured of a regular income, there was no point in even asking her.

Had Wally only been able to grow a beard. A nice, full, imperious, authoritative beard.

Then perhaps he would never have run off to join the army to become an army surgeon, and then a bacteriologist, and then director of the U.S. Army commission which unraveled the mystery of yellow fever, and finally the distinguished figure for whom the famous army medical center in Washington, D.C., is named.

For the University of Virginia's youngest-ever M.D., the peach-fuzz physician who may have missed out on a magnificent private practice by a whisker, was Walter Reed.

Now you know THE REST OF THE STORY.

74. Deadly Melody

In 510 B.C. the splendid Greek city of Sybaris was destroyed. It was the result of a war with another Greek city called Croton. Crotoniate troops took no prisoners, and all Sybarites who were unable to escape were murdered where they stood. Since the orders were total destruction, soldiers were seventy days—more than two months—demolishing the city. And if that weren't enough, says one ancient historian, after the remaining rubble was burned a nearby river was redirected over the smoldering waste, thus to bury forever even the site on which Sybaris had stood!

It would take twenty-five centuries and some fairly sophisticated technology to rediscover that site. But what could have inspired such hatred of one Greek city for another, especially for one as glorious as Sybaris? And how could the army of Croton possibly have defeated the army of Sybaris, outnumbered three to one?

Today, when one is called a "Sybarite," it means he is devoted to the good life, to luxury in the extreme. The term is derivative of the ancient Greek city of Sybaris, more directly of its pampered inhabitants.

For their Easy Street address, the original Sybarites were envied far and wide. But seeds of their extinction were sown inside the city walls.

The citizens who had it good became jealous of the citizens who had it better. One particularly eloquent troublemaker named Telys began making speeches. In fact, he actually persuaded the Sybarite tribunal to confiscate all the wealth and all the real estate of the five hundred richest men in town! Had the government only left those five hundred men alone, Sybaris might have survived the centuries. As it happened, you can barely find the place with a magnetometer!

The five hundred disenfranchised Sybarites fled to the city of Croton, seventy-five miles away. Hot on their heels, Sybarite messengers with an ultimatum for Croton: Return the five hundred or risk war.

As far as the Crotoniate assembly was concerned, war with powerful Sybaris was out of the question. The Sybarite army outnumbered the Crotoniate army three to one. So the Crotoniates were about to send those five hundred disenfranchised fat cats back to Sybaris when a distinguished gentleman addressed the assembly. He was the great mathematician, Pythagoras, who had been living in Croton for almost twenty years. Anyway, Pythagoras convinced the assembly to grant asylum to the displaced Sybarites and then to dispatch a corps of diplomats to Sybaris for a nice friendly chat.

The Crotoniates sent thirty such peaceful emissaries.

Upon their arrival in Sybaris, all were killed. That is the reason why Croton went against the odds, declared war on Sybaris with little hope of winning.

Of course, Croton did win. History records that Sybaris was utterly annihilated.

But the Crotoniates killed them softly—with a song! So far as we know, nothing like it had ever happened before, nor has it happened since. . . .

When the Crotoniate army advanced to within arrows' range of the Sybarite cavalry, Crotoniate musicians, pipers, began playing a certain tune often performed during Sybarite parades.

The magnificent Sybarite horses had been trained to *dance* whenever that music was played. And now, in battle, the entire Sybarite cavalry was dancing, prancing, elegantly sidestepping, ignoring the frantic commands of the riders.

Thus were the Sybarite forces slaughtered, and thus did the opulent society of Sybaris sink into oblivion—defeated by a graceful melody.

Now you know THE REST OF THE STORY.

75. Adams for Granted

Is THE VICE-PRESIDENCY of the United States just so much political window dressing? Gerald Ford thinks so. The former president says Congress should review and extend the responsibilities of the vice-president.

Perhaps we have taken our nation's number-two men for granted. What schoolchild, for example, could name the first *vice*-president of the United States?

In fact, can *you* name him?

He was John Adams, and even in *his* day the vice-presidency was rather taken for granted.

John Adams became vice-president, officially, on April 21, 1789.

New York City was our nation's capital back then, and visitors from all over the country had gathered to watch the infant government take its first steps.

Adams was escorted to the Senate, was greeted at the door by John Langdon: "Sir, I have it in charge from the Senate to introduce you to the chair of this House and also to congratulate you on your appointment to the office of Vice-President of the United States of America."

Langdon obviously respected Adams. Yet, equally obviously, he underestimated the extent of Adams' authority.

Adams stood before the Senate. He began: "Unaccustomed to refuse any public service, however dangerous to my reputation or disproportioned to my talents, it would have been inconsistent to have adopted another maxim of conduct at this time . . ."

And the new vice-president was warmly applauded.

Yet, clearly, neither he nor the senators he addressed realized what the vice-presidency meant to the nation at that moment.

Among Adams' first orders of official business was to determine the proper protocol in sending and receiving messengers from the House of Representatives.

Hardly a historic determination. Perhaps even unworthy of John Adams' attention at that point in his political career.

Everyone was taking Vice-President Adams for granted, including Vice-President Adams himself, because apparently no one knew THE REST OF THE STORY. . . .

I refer you to section one of our Constitution: "In case of the removal of the President from office, or of his death, resignation, or inability to discharge the powers and duties of the said office, the same shall devolve on the Vice President . . ."

And yes, the Constitution was effective at that time, and yes, the electoral college had voted George Washington president. Yet, as of John Adams' inauguration as vice-president, George Washington was not even in town, would not even take his presidential oath of office until nine days later, April 30!

For those nine days, President-Elect George Washington was technically, legally unable to act as president.

So by the authority of our own Constitution, Vice-President John Adams was this nation's leader.

We took John Adams for granted.

We robbed him of his rightful title: first president of the United States!

76. The Coronation of Czar Peter III

CZAR PETER III of Russia was the grandson of Peter the Great. And that was the only great thing about him. In fact, the only remarkable thing that ever happened to Peter III was his coronation. But first, THE REST OF THE STORY.

In December of 1741, thirteen-year-old Peter was designated as successor to the Russian throne. His mother's sister, Empress Elizabeth, made the decree. Had Peter's aunt known how the boy was going to turn out, she might have taken more time to consider who the next czar would be.

Four years later, Elizabeth commanded Peter to marry Princess Sophia Augusta Frederica. He was seventeen, she a year younger. And there ended any similarity between the two.

Princess Sophia was brilliant, irrepressible, fun-loving. Peter was dim-witted, puny, moody, childlike in every negative sense of the term. And he became czar in 1762, age thirty-three.

The responsibility of governing Russia, Peter delegated to the court nobility, which explains the subsequent volume of legislation favoring the nobility. Among other special privileges, noblemen were relieved of compulsory military service.

Peter had a talent for getting on people's nerves. He infuriated the clergy by allowing the government to intrude on church prerogatives. He even managed to alienate the one friend on whom he might have counted—his wife, Sophia. She tolerated Peter's threats of divorce, his aberrant behavior. The one thing she could not accept was her husband's disloyalty to Russia.

The problem was Peter's identification crisis with the king of Prussia, Frederick the Great. Peter probably would have given all of Russia to Frederick, granted enough time. Sophia made certain that her husband, the czar, had as little time as possible.

With her aid—some say by her orders—a *coup d'état* was launched against Peter. Only six months after inheriting the throne, Peter abdicated. A week later, he was assassinated.

There is considerable historical evidence that it was Peter's wife who had him rubbed out. Of course, she did become empress of Russia. You remember her, not by the name Sophia, but by the name she later chose: Catherine. The history books call her "Catherine the Great."

Mostly ignored as a bothersome twenty-six-week footnote is the reign of Catherine's husband, Peter III. Had he only been evil, he might have been interesting. In reality, he was a royal jerk. The only fascinating event of his career was his coronation. . . .

It was a splendid occasion, lasting more than three weeks. First, Peter was carried through the streets from the Convent of Saint Alexander Nevsky to the Cathedral of Saints Peter and Paul. As priests chanted, the czar ascended his throne and was presented with the imperial crown. Catherine was at his side all the while. In fact, Peter's coronation was one of the few things they shared.

Did I mention that, at the time, neither Peter nor Catherine was alive?

For when Catherine the Great passed away, her son Paul commanded that his father's body be exhumed—and that he, the otherwise undistinguished Peter III, be placed on his throne and crowned czar of all Russia in the presence of his wife's lifeless corpse.

Paul, who had always held his mother responsible for his

father's assassination, made this declaration: "In life divided, in death united."

And so did Czar Peter III win his place in history, after all.

He was the world's only monarch ever to be crowned thirty-four years after his death!

77. Captain Nice

BARTHOLOMEW ROBERTS WAS AN old-time sea captain.

Yet if your conception of what an old-time sea captain is supposed to be includes being boisterous, rough-talking, hard-drinking, irreverent, then maybe you'd better hear THE REST OF THE STORY.

Once upon a time, ship's musicians were among the hardest-working crew members. Like the family physicians of long ago, they were always "on call." If anyone aboard ship wanted music, at any time of day or night, the ship's orchestra was required to provide music.

The man who changed all that was Captain Bartholomew Roberts. Aboard his ships, the *Fortune*, the *Good Fortune*, and the *Royal Fortune*, the musicians were not only allowed but obliged to take Sunday off.

You see, Captain Roberts' background was conservative Welsh. He was a strict Sabbatarian. Once a week on every cruise, religious services were conducted.

Temperance was another of Captain Roberts' convictions. The hours during which crew members could drink beverages containing alcohol were carefully regulated. Alcoholism, or even common intoxication, was positively prohibited. As for himself, Captain Roberts drank tea. *Only* tea.

Games were permitted aboard—unless money was involved. Any form of gambling was against regulations. In fact, the captain frowned on games such as cards or dice, simply because those games were generally associated with gambling.

There is no record of a woman ever having been smuggled aboard any of Captain Roberts' vessels by any member of his crew. The reason is obvious. The captain made it clear that any member guilty of such immoral behavior would be hanged.

I don't know if Captain Roberts ever conducted a bed check of those serving under him. There was, however, a standing order: lights out by 8:00 P.M.

Of course, no fighting was allowed. This was the way Captain Roberts handled it: If two crew members had a quarrel which could not be resolved through discussion, they were required to wait until the ship had reached port, then to settle their dispute on land in a fair fight refereed by the ship's quartermaster. Under no circumstances was such violence to be permitted on board any vessel commanded by Captain Roberts.

If this discipline was remarkable for the high seas of the early eighteenth century, Roberts himself was a remarkable man, always superbly groomed, splendidly attired. He wore a rich crimson damask waistcoat and trousers, a red feather in his tricorn hat, two pairs of pistols on the end of a silk sling over his shoulders, a gleaming sword at his side, and a gold chain suspending a diamond cross around his neck.

Captain Bartholomew Roberts.

Those serving in his command called him "pistol-proof," a phrase used to describe only the most adept in ship handling, crew control, and the tactics of naval warfare.

No telling the greatness he might have achieved on the right side of wrong.

For Captain Bartholomew Roberts was a strict Sabbatarian, a teetotaler, a gentle man who disapproved of fast money and loose women. He was Mr. Discipline, Captain Nice. And he captured more than four hundred ships during one four-year period in his career.

As a *pirate*.

One of the most feared—and often considered the greatest—pirate in the history of piracy.

Bartholomew Roberts.

The original "Black Bart."

78. Two Loves, One Hate

Miss C. A. Moore. Call her Amy. An intense, strong-willed young lady. "Hardheaded," her parents so often said.

With her natural tenacity, Amy should have succeeded brilliantly at life. Instead, she was destined for unhappiness.

The reason was two failed marriages. The culprit in both cases: alcohol. Booze cost Amy her first husband *and* her second.

Amy was not quite nineteen when a handsome young man knocked at her parents' door. He was Dr. Charles Gloyd, physician, linguist, scholar. A newcomer to Belton, Missouri, he asked if Amy's folks would mind taking in a boarder. They were delighted. That is, in the beginning.

For it was as a captain in the Uncivil War that Dr. Gloyd began drinking heavily. The war stopped. The doctor did not.

Amy's mother and dad often heard him stumbling in late at night. Amy never heard, or perhaps refused to hear.

For Amy was falling in love. Worse still, so was Dr. Gloyd.

Forbidden to be alone in the same room together, the sweethearts were driven to subterfuge, to secret love notes and clandestine meetings. The more her parents objected, the more determined Amy became to pursue the romance.

And so it was, on November 21, 1867, that Amy and Dr. Gloyd were married.

The groom arrived at the ceremony—drunk.

Stubborn Amy clung to the hope that her love might reform her beloved. They moved to the town of Holden in Johnson County. Charles tried to establish a practice there. But whenever prospective patients came calling, the doctor was usually out pouring it in or in sleeping it off.

In his ever infrequent hours of sobriety, Charles was changing, was growing moody, distant, eventually outright cold. And the worst was yet to come.

Amy was pregnant. She became a living caricature of the drunkard's wife—a pathetic, malnourished creature, roaming the chilly streets with a tattered shawl clutched at her bosom.

Timidly venturing into dark hangouts, Amy begged the barkeeps to stop selling to her husband. More often than not they would laugh at her. At home she wept incessantly. And waited. And wondered what kind of world this was into which she would soon bring her child.

Amy's father rescued her just in time, took her back home to Belton, where she gave birth to a baby girl.

The infant's own daddy was dead of his excesses less than a year later.

I wish there were some sort of happy ending to relate. Amy did marry again, a minister named David, although, as you'll recall, I mentioned that booze broke up that relationship too. More precisely, Amy's bitterness about booze . . .

For Pastor David, himself a teetotaler, simply could not get used to his wife's harping on the issue, her constant crusading against Demon Rum.

Finally, when her vendetta took her too far from the home fires, the clergyman divorced her. The grounds: desertion.

History tells us about a tall, powerful woman who spent much of her life devastating saloons with a hatchet. Her raids became world-renowned. She—Carry Amelia Moore—naturally used the name of her second husband, Pastor David *Nation*.

You have always known the name Carry Nation.

Now you know THE REST OF THE STORY.

79. Britain's National Asset

IT HAD BEGUN as a world's fair exhibition hall. It would be recognized as an architectural wonder, a national asset to Great Britain.

Morton Shand would describe it as "a precept inspiring as the Parthenon, an exemplar vital as the Pont du Gard . . . as important as Stonehenge or Ely Cathedral."

Made almost entirely of glass, it was called the Crystal Palace. Its glory is THE REST OF THE STORY.

In the summer of 1850, it was decided that the Great International Exhibition would be held in London's Hyde Park. Not merely in Hyde Park, but in a magnificent building unlike any ever constructed.

Originally it was conceived as a huge structure of bricks and mortar. Designer Joseph Paxton suggested iron and glass. His plans were accepted.

The first column was erected September 26.

Long before its completion, the building was being hailed as a national asset. In November, the publication *Punch* nicknamed it the "Crystal Palace." The name stuck.

A brief workers' strike and two torrential storms slowed construction. Still, the last pane of glass was in place in January 1851. London's press and public were ecstatic. As the months passed, the colossal, shining edifice inspired extraordinary pride nationwide.

The Crystal Palace—the building itself—covered almost twenty acres. The main section was about two thousand feet long, four hundred feet wide, and a hundred feet high. That's not counting a thousand-foot-long addition on the north end.

There were three entrances, seventeen exits, and ten double stairways to the galleries.

Five thousand tons of iron, six hundred thousand cubic feet of timber, and a third of a million glass panes were used. It would require twenty-four miles of guttering to carry water away from the roof.

The ingenious architecture included interchangeable structures. Many of the twenty-three hundred girders and thirty-three thousand columns were prefabricated so that one might be substituted for another.

Three large elm trees, which were growing in Hyde Park before the Crystal Palace construction had begun, were left inside the mammoth exhibition hall. An arched glass transept was constructed to cover those magnificent trees.

Fourteen thousand exhibitors displayed over a hundred thousand exhibits. For the people of Britain, one display eclipsed all the others—the beautiful, breathtaking Crystal Palace itself.

When the exhibition was over, the public could not bear to see the Crystal Palace demolished. It was removed, column by column, pane by pane, all twenty acres of it, to nearby Sydenham. There, in South London, was to be its permanent home.

Decades passed. Decades of shows and exhibitions and festivals.

The great towers survived a devastating fire in the autumn of 1936.

They were all that survived.

Yet so fond were the memories of all the wonder-filled yesterdays that those towers were carefully, lovingly preserved, forever to be cherished as glittering reminders of an age gone by.

Forever lasted until the winter of 1940 and the bombing of London.

And then somebody realized the Nazi bombers were following a beacon no blackout could dim. The gleaming Crystal Palace towers, glistening brightly even by moonlight, had become a surefire, round-the-clock London landmark for the German air raids.

One of the nation's greatest assets had become a monumental national liability.

And so, in 1941, the British demolished the magnificent towers of the Crystal Palace. Not the Nazis, the *British*.

What they destroyed was not the beloved architectural treasure, but the silent, shining betrayer.

Not the beauty.

The beast.

80. The Test Market

THERE IS A WHOLE LOT MORE to psychiatry than sexual motivations and dream interpretations these days. In fact, over the past three decades the Freudians have been slowly squeezed out of the psychiatric picture by a new approach.

This promising fledgling science is psychopharmacology. Where psychoanalysis has failed, chemicals are opening the doors to the mind.

This next is a close look at one "modern miracle" psychotropic substance, a soft, silver-white, metallic chemical element, actually the lightest known metal: lithium.

It was about the middle of the nineteenth century when doctors began to suspect that lithium was good for something besides chemical categorization. Precisely what, they were not sure. Because of its chemical interaction with uric acid in the laboratory, it was hoped that lithium would prove successful in treating gout and rheumatism. It did not. Some reported salutory effects on diabetic patients. It turned out they were wrong.

Then, in 1948, an Australian psychiatrist named John Cade, working alone in a mental hospital laboratory, performed the pioneer research which would later be recognized as the origin of psychopharmacology. The mind-altering substance with which Cade experimented was lithium.

Toxicity was the initial obstacle. Yet, to Cade, the potential benefits seemed to outweigh the risks. After lab animals, he dosed himself with lithium carbonate and lithium citrate. Finally he administered lithium to ten mental patients suffering from manic disorders. The conditions of all ten improved dramatically.

Clinicians in the United States, while not contesting Cade's results, were still skeptical of lithium's potential because of the hazards involved in its use. But as the years passed, so did lithium's image—from poison almost all the way to panacea.

It was 1969 before its clinical application was more than a rare occasion. Finally, in 1970, the FDA officially approved lithium for the treatment of manic disorders. Today, of course, the spectrum of psychotropic medications includes many specifically effective drugs. And yet lithium, as a treatment and preventive for certain psychoses, will perhaps always have its place.

Almost twenty years before the experiments of psychiatrist John Cade, there was what you might call a test market for lithium as a psychotropic. In any event, slogans ascribed to the product certainly suggested its calming effect on the hyperexcitable.

All John Cade would have had to do was ask a Saint Louis businessman named Charles L. Grigg to report the favorable results he had observed—in his customers. But wouldn't you know? Just as the world of psychiatry began discovering the psychotropic power of lithium, someone objected and made Charlie Grigg stop putting it in his popular concoction.

Why, it's been more than thirty years since that nice little company in Saint Louis listed lithium among the ingredients—in Seven-Up.

Now you know THE REST OF THE STORY.

81. The Misfortunes of Mahlon Loomis

FALSE TEETH. The mineral-plating process for making false teeth has a U.S. patent dated May 1854.

There is also a subsequent British patent held by the same inventor, a Philadelphia dentist named Mahlon Loomis. Mahlon Loomis invented the "kaolin" process for making dentures.

As any inventor might tell you, a patent isn't everything. In fact, Mahlon Loomis is a mostly forgotten man.

He came from a distinguished family, was well educated, had a thriving dental practice. He was also clever and inventive, and that complicated his life.

He was in his early thirties when he began tinkering with the invention for which few remember him.

The dentist labored for most of a decade during his spare time, was in his forties before he felt his pet project was ready to be shared with the rest of the world.

Mahlon called a meeting of scientists in Virginia, and before that eminent audience he demonstrated his discovery.

Loomis' invention was greeted with unanimous enthusiasm.

After the back patting was finished and the scientists had gone home, the money men moved in. Boston capitalists approached the inventive dentist and proposed that they all get rich.

That was fine with Mahlon.

But then came September 24, 1869, a day of unprecedented panic on Wall Street. They called it Black Friday, and there would be nothing like it until the crash of 1929.

At any rate, the economic upheaval broke Loomis' Boston backers. The dentist decided to wait out the Wall Street storm and find other investors.

After two years, Mahlon tired of waiting for the East Coast to come around, and he found some eager bankers in Chicago. The dentist was really onto something, the bankers said. They would gladly put their money where Mahlon's mouth was.

That encouraging news came in the first week of October 1871.

You know what happened in the second week? The Great Chicago Fire. And once more, Mahlon Loomis' prospective investors were wiped out, this time almost literally!

Even the United States government tried to assist the hapless dentist. Economic assistance, in the form of a "Loomis Bill," passed the House in May of 1872 and the Senate in January of 1873. President Grant even signed the bill. Problem was, by the time the bill had gone through legislation, Mahlon's money appropriation had been legislated out. In the end, the whole thing amounted to little more than congratulations.

Mahlon died in 1886—heartbroken, they say, over his nation's failure to recognize him.

The mineral-plating process for making false teeth? Mahlon wasn't concerned about that. It was his other invention in which Mahlon held his highest hopes. The invention of wireless telegraphy.

That invention history credits to Marconi. Only a Philadelphia dentist named Mahlon Loomis gave his first public demonstration, conducting a two-way wireless communication at a distance of eighteen miles—six years before Marconi was born!

Now you know THE REST OF THE STORY.

82. Nice Catch

WHAT YOU ARE ABOUT TO READ happened on Sunday, July 26, 1981, at 7:30 in the morning.

Tom and Lorri Deal, asleep in their apartment in suburban Chicago, awakened to hear a baby crying. The crying continued for quite some while. For so long, in fact, that young Tom eventually got out of bed to investigate.

From his bedroom window he could see the apartment building across the parking lot. And the balconies of that building. And on one of those third-floor balconies, the sliding screen door was partly open. And a months-old baby was crawling out onto the balcony and toward the balustrade.

Tom Deal knew no one whom he might telephone in that apartment building. So the twenty-two-year-old warehouseman threw on his robe and dashed downstairs and across the parking lot.

Directly above him he could still hear the baby crying. Frantically he rang the door buzzer of the apartment, hoping to awaken someone inside. He rang the buzzer for five minutes before giving up.

By now the baby had reached the balustrade, the row of upright iron posts supporting the balcony railing. If Tom was not completely awake before, he was now.

For ever so slowly, the baby stretched one leg between the balusters and then dangled that leg over the edge of the balcony.

Tom shouted, "No, go back!"

No use.

Moments later, another plump little leg appeared.

Now not even calling for help would help. For by the time anyone had broken down the door to that apartment, it would be too late. Tom just knew it. The baby was going to fall. And all Tom could do in the sweaty panic of those agonizing seconds was stretch out his arms—and pray.

And the baby did slip between the balusters . . .

And topple from the third-story balcony . . .

And graze the second-floor balcony railing . . .

And tumble forward and down, into the arms of young Tom Deal!

The baby, ten-month-old Jennifer, was still crying but safe. Tom took her to a nearby hospital emergency room to make sure she was all right, and she was all right. All she needed was a diaper change.

Local police investigated the case of this apparently neglected infant. They discovered a baby-sitter had waited until three o'clock that morning for the child's mother to return home. Then the baby-sitter took little Jennifer to this other apartment. Because there was no crib, the infant was left sleeping on a couch. At 7:30 A.M. little Jennifer awakened, crawled over to the balcony sliding screen door which was not locked, and crawled out.

That's how it happened.

But this is THE REST OF THE STORY.

Saturday, the day before, rescuer Tom Deal was playing softball.

He often plays softball on summer Saturdays.

You have just read about the phenomenal catch he made the morning after—ten-month-old Jennifer, who had fallen three stories from the apartment balcony.

Nice catch.

But Tom's no catcher. Ask any of his teammates. Tom Deal is a chronic butterfingers.

For on Saturday, the day before he caught when it really counted, Tom flubbed a fly ball softball costing his team five runs!

83. The Ahosi

THE JUNGLE IS QUIET. The villagers are asleep. It is an hour before dawn.

Suddenly and from every direction an army attacks the village. There are thousands of African soldiers. They have remained undetected by silently cutting a narrow path through the jungle and then surrounding the village before any of its inhabitants have awakened.

Surprise is the trademark of this fighting force, among the most feared on the entire continent. They are the Ahosi, a regiment of the greater army of the African nation of Dahomey.

For the village under attack, there is not the slightest hope—although none will be killed unless he resists the Ahosi. For the economy of the nation of Dahomey depends almost entirely on the slave trade. The objective of the Ahosi warriors, in this case, is to capture all of the villagers unharmed and then transport them to the coast where they will be sold as slaves.

What you have just read really happened. Innumerable times. A European traveler once observed that the Ahosi were "savage as wounded gorillas, more cruel far than their brethren in arms."

What made the Ahosi such special soldiers is THE REST OF THE STORY.

Dahomey's King Agadga was first to organize the spectacular regiment. That was in the early 1700s. Reportedly, its first assignment was to attack and destroy the combined armies of two neighboring nations. The king's regiment succeeded.

The people of Dahomey often referred to them as "Meno" warriors. The formal designation was "Ahosi."

Ahosi was a name that caused the brave to tremble in those days.

In 1818, King Ghezo ascended to the throne. For eighty years Dahomey had been paying tribute to one of the powerful Yoruba states. Dahomey's new king declared this an indignity and determined the solution to be war.

It was he, King Ghezo, who made his nation's army one of the most awesome in Africa. He gave special attention to the Ahosi, the rugged regiment which had served past kings so well.

You could have seen the Ahosi coming a mile away if they had wanted you to. Their uniforms were distinctive. They wore blue-and-white-striped sleeveless coats and short trousers.

The soldiers specialized within the regiment. First the grenadiers, the biggest and strongest of the troops. If it exploded, they knew how to use it. In fact, each of the grenadiers was attended by an ammunition bearer.

Then the "elephant hunters," recognized as the bravest of the troops. Each of these soldiers, it was said, could bring down seven elephants with one volley.

And the archers, the flashy parade corps, all no less deadly with their silent weapons. And, of course, the infantry, the hingepin of the Ahosi forces. One wonders if King Ghezo could have succeeded against his Yoruban enemy without them.

The military supremacy of the Ahosi was long and glorious, but the ferocious regiment of African warriors met its match in 1892 in the army of France.

I don't believe I mentioned that the Ahosi, the terror of Africa for almost two hundred years, popularly called "Meno," were not men at all.

Meno, in the language of Dahomey, means "our mothers." Ahosi, the term which literally describes what they were, means "the wives of the king."

That ruthless fighting force was actually comprised of the king's wives!

84. The Big Picture

IT HAPPENED IN POLAND in 1794. And it was something to celebrate. In fact, it was such a joyous event that almost a hundred years would pass and the Polish people would plan to begin the celebration all over again.

With a painting.

Not with just any painting, but with something called a "cyclorama"—a giant painting, forty-two feet high and four hundred feet long!

The man behind the idea was Polish artist Jan Styka.

In 1891, as the centennial approached, Jan had completed a small painting called *Polonia*, which commemorated the happy happening. Then he decided it was not enough. Such a glorious occurrence required more spectacular homage. That's when Jan made up his mind he would enlarge upon the little painting until it encompassed the full significance of the occasion.

In January of 1893, one year before the centennial, a Polish citizens committee was formed to raise money for the project. The *Panorama of Raclawice*, as it was being called, was to be exhibited in its own building, and architect Ludwik Ramult would undertake the design.

Meanwhile, Jan Styka and a fellow artist named Kossak visited the site at which the grand event had occurred. Now they had the "feel." But neither artist had ever painted a cyclorama before. So Jan traveled to Munich for a crash course in panorama painting.

April 4, Jan was back in Poland, meeting with Kossak and

two historians. With so much time and energy invested in the project thus far, the content of the work must be absolutely historically accurate.

By the end of the month, preliminary sketches were submitted to and approved by the citizens committee. It would take Styka and Kossak and six other artists to transfer the sketches to that monster forty-two-by-four-hundred-foot canvas.

The panorama was completed thirteen months later, and its exhibition was opened to the public June 5, 1894. The centennial festivities were officially under way.

The remarkable artwork would remain on display in the city of Lvov for fifty years. Then, in 1944, the war. The panorama's exhibition hall was bombed. The panorama itself was damaged. Fearing the magnificent painting's complete destruction, curators removed it and hid it in a monastery.

When the war was over, the Polish people begged their government to restore their beloved masterwork and to display it once more. Such pleas were continually refused.

A decade ago permission was finally granted by the Polish government. A rotunda for the *Panorama of Raclawice* would be constructed in Wroclaw.

Donations poured in from all over Poland.

The construction was well under way when suddenly permission was withdrawn, and the half-built building lay dormant for many years. But in 1980, the Polish government gave the go-ahead for the rotunda's completion. Again, in spite of the nation's weakening economy, donations poured in. And the magnificent panorama emerged from hiding, borne in huge rolls in a caravan of trucks, greeted by jubilant crowds as it passed through each community. The giant *Panorama of Raclawice* has returned—maybe just in time.

For that painting, a symbol of the Poles' determination to be free, has cheered them on as has the event which it represents, now almost two centuries past.

At the very least, the panorama has come back to haunt the Polish people. For it depicts the Polish uprising in 1794 against the forces of occupation, the rule of *Russia*.

And by the way . . .

The Poles won!

Now you know THE REST OF THE STORY.

85. The Jerk

IT WAS IN THE SPRING OF 1922 that the students began complaining about their postal service.

The University of Mississippi had its own United States post office, right there on campus. The students picked up and posted their own mail at that office.

The problem was the postmaster.

He was a jerk.

Bill did not want the job in the first place. Friends convinced him he needed the job, pulled some strings for him. Bill took a civil service exam, passed somehow, and became U.S. postmaster for the University of Mississippi.

One wonders how much of his personal history was recorded on his application.

Bill was a high school dropout, a U.S. Army reject, a college dropout, in that order. It was at "Ole Miss" that he managed finally to get accepted, but where he failed to complete his freshman year.

Now he was back, age twenty-four, in the nonacademic position of campus postmaster.

The solemn responsibility of being an employee of the United States government never really dawned on Bill. And he never really appreciated how easy the job was.

Another postal employee transported the incoming and outgoing mail between the train station and the post office. That left Bill with sorting the mail and selling stamps, and that was about it. But even that was too much for him.

Earliest complaints were that it took Bill too long to *begin* sorting the incoming mail. There were often long lines of restless students outside the post office.

In even more direct ways Bill was a public relations failure.

His attitude toward post office patrons ranged from indifferent to hostile. Back there behind the window he always seemed to be sitting down, frequently engaged in reading a magazine which had been mailed to someone else.

One of the few times he actually spoke, it was to say that he did not intend to beat the beck and call of every expletive-deleted who had two cents to buy a stamp.

Pretty soon, Bill was spending more and more time away from the post office. According to one reliable source, he used to walk around staring at trees "as though studying each leaf."

Brooding is what he was doing.

Then the final indignity.

It wasn't enough that he was slow in fulfilling what duties he had, that he was cold and sometimes even nasty to his patrons, that he neglected even the basic responsibility of staying on the post office premises. Bill actually began *throwing away the mail.*

Students and faculty members could often be found rummaging through the post office trash cans in search of personal and official correspondence.

It took U.S. postal authorities almost three years to get rid of Bill. That he was not ultimately thrown into jail was credited to one government inspector with a sense of humor.

You might envision such a young man winding up shoveling coal. And Bill did wind up shoveling coal at a Mississippi power plant. When he failed at that, he did the only thing that was left. He became an author and won the Pulitzer Prize.

Twice.

The Mississippi postmaster who threw away the mail was *William Faulkner.*

Now you know THE REST OF THE STORY.

86. Heaven on Skis

ARABELLA WILLIAMS IS NOT just another southern California sexpot searching the beaches for boys. Her fascination with the water is mostly sport, specifically, water-skiing.

Arabella is a superb water-skier. Been at it fifteen years.

On her second try she was water-borne on two skis. Quickly she graduated to one ski, which has remained her style ever since.

Arabella has tons of trophies. New Year's Day 1982 she won her eighth polar-bear trophy for her skiing performance in the near-freezing water of San Diego's Mission Bay. That's without a wet suit, incidentally. Arabella was quoted as saying the water "felt great."

She claims jogging provides the best physical conditioning for her sport, and so she jogs regularly. She used to ice-skate and play tennis and basketball. Now there is little recreation time for anything but water-skiing.

Arabella fits the California girl picture so precisely in most ways that you would never guess she was born in Chicago.

She is a health-food purist. Her diet is one of whole grains and fresh fruits and raw vegetables, food so rich in nutrition that she needs no vitamin supplements. She strictly denies herself fats and oils.

Her water-skiing injuries have all been minor ones because, as she says, she takes no chances. For instance, she never skis double with another skier. She considers that very dangerous.

Partly responsible for her safety record is her remarkable

grace. Indeed, she is heaven on skis. And yet, calling her that, I really must relate THE REST OF THE STORY.

Arabella does not spend her life garnering trophies for water-skiing.

Watching her, would you ever imagine that Arabella Williams is also a missionary? Well, she is.

She has ministered to the natives of Peru and Brazil. And she continues to travel around the world to help where help is needed.

Working through her Seventh-Day Adventist church group, she has made fifteen such journeys to help build churches and schools and hospitals. I mean physically to help build those buildings!

She has roofed and sided and painted and tiled from Baja to North Dakota to the Canadian Yukon. In 1981, Arabella helped build the superstructure of a ship, a vessel to sail the Amazon River bearing medical aid to the poor.

So Arabella Williams is a missionary—with a hobby.

After grappling with heavy equipment at construction sites all over the globe, water-skiing is hardly a challenge. But it is a relaxation, even for one whose mission in life is a divine one.

Arabella Williams is heaven on skis, not merely for the graceful execution of her sport but for the inspiration she offers daily, perhaps largely unwittingly.

There is so much to think about that Arabella rarely if ever ponders her age.

Arabella Williams, the vigorous Seventh-Day Adventist missionary who has spent much of her past fifteen years water-skiing, continues to win trophies doing so.

At *eighty-five*.

87. A Shadow Called Jane

No one ever saw the lady of the house. In fact, some playfully suggested that she did not exist at all, knowing full well she was there, shut up in her bedroom with the draperies closed tightly.

Physically, there was nothing wrong with Jane.

Many years before, she had had tuberculosis. She was frail and small, with thin pencil-line features, not sturdy at all. But medically, there was no reason for Jane's total seclusion. It was simply the life she chose. And this is THE REST OF THE STORY.

In the winter of that year, on January 6, the family was returning by rail from Boston to their home in Concord, New Hampshire. There was eleven-year-old Benny, his daddy Frank and his mommy Jane.

Jane was quite a protective mother, and with profound reason. She had already lost two children. Her first son had died in infancy, her second at the age of four. Benny, her third son, was now an only child, and Jane watched over him carefully.

The train was traveling at full speed en route to Concord when it happened. An axle on one of the passenger cars sheered off, and the crippled coaches, helplessly linked, tumbled down a steep embankment.

There were cries of confusion and pain. After the crash, Frank pulled himself from the twisted rubble. Jane, still at his side, was also bruised but otherwise unharmed.

It was as though eleven-year-old Benny had vanished. Obviously the boy had been thrown elsewhere in the coach as it toppled from the track.

Frank called out, "Benny!" No answer. Frank searched. And then he saw . . .

The child's body lay crumpled in the wreckage. The back of his head was gone.

Suddenly livid, Frank threw a shawl over the lifeless form, although not in time. Jane had caught a glimpse of Benny and, horror-struck, screamed. In an instant Jane's world was obliterated. The years left to her would be virtually devoid of reality.

Frank assured his wife that they would have a new home and a new life. There would be nothing to remind them of their loss.

The first day in that new home, Jane went upstairs to her bedroom and shut the door. And there she stayed.

A devoutly religious person, Jane perceived what had happened as a judgment from God. Overwhelmed by guilt, she handwrote letters to her dead son, begging his forgiveness for any attention she might have failed to pay, any love she might have failed to show.

Meanwhile, Frank frantically attempted to console his wife. It was not right for her to withdraw like this, he insisted. It was not healthy. Jane must come out into the sunlight now and breathe the fresh air and put all the anguish behind her. But the melancholy woman would not respond to her husband's urgings. And she kept the world locked out for two years.

Jane never fully recovered from her grief. She wore black inside and out for the rest of her life. The few social functions she attended she infected with her morbidity.

I am glad you've met Jane. She has given you another perspective on a position you might have believed always enviable. For if you are happy in your life, whatever your life, you have won.

Jane hated her husband's profession, was haunted by

death and by guilt, even though the new home in which she was solitarily confined was the most prestigious in the country.

The newspapers called her "the shadow in the White House."

She was the wife of President Franklin Pierce.

The First Lady of the land.

88. The Spiritualist

ARTHUR WAS A CATHOLIC turned atheist turned agnostic.

Many who knew him sincerely wished he had left it at that.

But there was one more area of belief into which Arthur would pass, and from which he would never return:

Spiritualism.

In fact, Arthur became so devout in his religion of communication with the dead that he is recognized, even to this day, as one of the most outspoken and outstanding spiritualists of all time.

When Arthur made public his "conversion" to spiritualism, he lost a great many friends—folks who had perceived him as a broad-shouldered, clearheaded apostle of common sense, the consummate logician. Yet such was his passionate enthusiasm for this wondrous new preoccupation that he made every imaginable sacrifice to spread what he considered the good news: The dead are not dead.

Critics were everywhere.

Traditional theists attacked him as a spokesman for Satan. He once received a letter addressed to "Chief Devil, Spiritualist Church." Spiritualism, ministers warned, was based on Lucifer's first lie: "Thou shalt not surely die."

Arthur defended himself as best he could. But no sooner had he crossed swords with established religion than another, even more formidable, group opposed him.

They were the professional magicians.

There was nothing a séance medium could do that a

magician could not do better. In fact, most magicians were offended by the pathetically uncomplicated tricks used by mediums to deceive their patrons. Magicians contended that the victims of professional spiritualism believed primarily because they wanted so badly to believe.

Yet for all of the criticism heaped upon Arthur, he was never accused of insincerity, nor of being in it for the money.

Personally independently wealthy, he accepted only expenses for his spiritualist lectures, every penny of profit above which was donated to the cause of spiritualism.

Arthur's series of seven lectures at New York City's Carnegie Hall was a sellout record-breaker. The effectiveness of his message could be seen in the widespread rash of suicides which followed. Arthur had made the next world sound so vastly preferable to this one that a great many Manhattanites simply could not wait to get there.

One woman drank the contents of a bottle of Lysol, convinced she would be in a better position to assist her husband once she had reached the Other Side. No record survives to suggest whether her husband agreed. In either case, the poison took a week to kill her, during which time the woman busied herself with exotic funeral arrangements.

In another instance, a young man killed himself, proclaiming that there were "no gas bills in the Hereafter."

And the suicide notes which littered the town, virtually all of them, had one thing in common: an expression of gratitude—to Arthur.

What is truly miraculous about Arthur's spiritualist "ministry" is that it did not obliterate his previous accomplishments.

And lest we judge him too harshly, it ought not to be forgot—Arthur meant no harm.

He was merely romantic, idealistic, curious, and hopeful. And perhaps one thing more: He could not tolerate an unsolvable riddle.

For Arthur was a mystery writer—who sought to unravel the ultimate mystery.

Sir Arthur *Conan Doyle,* creator of the unstumpable sleuth, Sherlock Holmes!

Now you know THE REST OF THE STORY.

89. Invisible Eddie

IT WAS THE DEAD of night, precisely one-thirty on a chilly December morning, when Mrs. Lilly was awakened by the creaking of a door.

Eyes wide in the blackness, she called out, "Who's there?"

Silence.

Instantly the woman's throat went dry.

A common intruder, well, that would be one thing. But for two years now members of the household had felt an unseen presence, as though someone or something was always nearby, lurking, hiding, watching.

In moments Mrs. Lilly's eyes had adjusted to the dark, just in time to see the door to the adjoining room open slowly. It was a terrible, deliberate slowness with which a door might move had it a mind of its own.

Once more, only much louder this time, "Who's there?"

Again, no answer.

Then suddenly the door slammed shut.

Mrs. Lilly shot bolt-upright in bed, perspiration dotting her forehead. Whatever it was, it was in the next room.

Quickly the woman sprang up and locked the door.

Louise, who had been asleep in her own room down the hall, rushed in when she heard Mrs. Lilly call for help. Informed of what had happened, Louise courageously suggested they unlock the door and inspect the room.

Mrs. Lilly agreed they must.

The door ajar, they could see the room was dark. Yet

when a lamp was lighted, nothing more was revealed. Just the furniture in the room. But no *one*.

So how, then, could the women account for that familiar, unmistakable feeling that their eyes were deceiving them—that indeed, although no one was seen, someone was there?

The "presence."

And now at once, a slight sound, something moving against the carpet—and the sound was coming from under the sofa!

Louise crept cautiously toward it, closer by inches, and when she was close enough to place both her hands on it, she pushed the sofa aside to expose *a young boy*.

And this is THE REST OF THE STORY.

The boy's name was Eddie Jones.

He was the chronic runaway son of a tailor who lived not far away. The household where he was discovered by Mrs. Lilly and Louise had become rather his second home.

And no one knew.

He actually lived there undetected, stealing food from the kitchen by night and hiding by day, the longest of his three stays lasting one uninterrupted year!

Repeatedly caught, Invisible Eddie returned. At last, when he was old enough, they sent him off to join the navy.

"Supposing he had come into the bedroom—how frightened I should have been!" declared Queen Victoria.

Or did I mention . . .

Louise was the *Baroness* Louise Lehzen.

And Mrs. Lilly was the queen's nurse.

And they all agreed, that chilly December morning in 1840, after invisible Eddie Jones had been captured in the queen's dressing room, that something really must be done to improve security—at Buckingham Palace.

90. The Day the Biltmore Burned

IN THE HISTORY OF Phoenix, Arizona, there have been several four-alarm fires, no five-alarm fires. Only one six-alarm fire.

The six-alarm happened in June 1973.

It summoned some 35 fire engines, ladders and pumpers, manned by 150 fire fighters.

Ablaze was the city's number-one world-famous landmark, the Arizona Biltmore Hotel.

The fire destroyed the fourth floor, damages estimated in the millions. But the money wasn't the main issue.

For the Arizona Biltmore, then forty-four years old, was an architectural masterpiece. Originally thought to have been the work of a little-known architect named Albert Chase McArthur, there is recent and profoundly convincing evidence that the Biltmore was originally designed by Frank Lloyd Wright.

In either case, the Biltmore architect was dead. And the reconstruction would require ultimately skilled, sensitive supervision.

Owners of the hotel agreed that only one architectural firm was specifically qualified: Taliesin West. Taliesin had been established for the purpose of perpetuating Frank Lloyd Wright's style, was in fact populated by Wright's own pupils. And no matter who sketched the elevation and floor plan, there is no question that the Biltmore's unique concrete-block construction was exclusively Frank Lloyd Wright's innovation.

Wright's students, therefore, must be the ones to restore the Biltmore.

And then the hotel owners told the Taliesin architects THE REST OF THE STORY.

The painstaking project which might have required years—the reconstruction of that precious landmark—must be accomplished in days.

The fire was in June 1973. The promised reopening date, September, same year. To miss the tourist season could mean bankruptcy.

Three months. Ninety days and nights before the beloved Biltmore would welcome guests once more.

Construction engineers argued the early deadline. Three months were just too few days for such an enormous task.

But the Biltmore owners could not survive both the tragic fire loss and a canceled winter season. Therefore began a round-the-clock workathon, a labor of love by the lovers of Frank Lloyd Wright. And love conquered all.

In ninety days the prestigious Arizona Biltmore was restored to her former glory. Unique paneling, gold-leaf ceiling, acid-cleaned or replaced stonework, original rococo moldings, lights buried in uniquely reticulated cement.

In a flurry of exhaustion, exhilaration, and celebration, the doors reopened on the twenty-ninth of September.

And that was the happy ending to the only six-alarm fire thus far in Phoenix history.

All during the reconstruction, of course, investigators sifted the evidence and eyewitness testimony to determine the fire's origin. This must never happen again, all agreed.

The first suspect was a carelessly tossed cigarette. Then it was suggested that a stretch of forty-four-year-old wiring had shorted out. Both of those notions were eventually dismissed.

Then the true cause of the fire was discovered.

Incredulous investigators checked and rechecked the facts. It couldn't be, could it?

Yet, unbelievable as it seemed, it had occurred just that way.

What started the Arizona Biltmore fire, the only six-alarm blaze in the city's history, was the arc of a welding torch of a welder who was installing an automatic fire-prevention sprinkler system!

91. Dewey Knew

LET'S SAY YOU ARE RUNNING for president. And you have information which would surely defeat the other fellow. But for you to publicize the information might jeopardize the security of our country.

Would you. speak out anyway, and win, or keep your mouth shut and lose?

At least one presidential candidate we know of was confronted with that dilemma.

In 1944, Tom Dewey was running for president against Franklin Delano Roosevelt. If he, Dewey, hoped to defeat the popular incumbent, he would need all the help he could get.

That summer, help arrived in the form of damaging information against his opponent. A shocked, disbelieving Dewey learned that U.S. Intelligence had cracked the Japanese secret code—in 1941. To him that meant that the United States knew in advance of the attack on Pearl Harbor, but that FDR had done nothing to prevent it.

Had the Republican candidate's source been less than reliable, I believe Dewey would have dismissed this information as the wishful thinking of some bitter fellow Republican. Dewey's source, however, was completely credible. He had to believe. Even though the thought of a U.S. president permitting a Pearl Harbor for any reason was thoroughly distasteful to Tom Dewey.

His first reaction was: The people must be told THE REST

OF THE STORY—that Franklin Roosevelt, to whet our appetites for war, allowed the Japanese to obliterate our base in the Hawaiian Islands.

Then, somehow, Army Chief-of-Staff George Marshall discovered that Dewey knew about the code.

September 26, Tom Dewey was campaigning, was staying briefly at a hotel in Tulsa, Oklahoma. He had not yet used his trump card.

Dewey was in his Tulsa hotel room. A knock at the door. Dewey answered. A man introduced himself as Colonel Carter Clarke, an army intelligence officer. He, Clarke, had been instructed to deliver a confidential message from George Marshall.

Dewey opened the sealed letter from the army chief-of-staff and read: "You understand the utterly tragic consequences if the present political debates regarding Pearl Harbor disclose to the public any suspicion of the vital sources of information we possess. The conduct of all operations in the Pacific are closely related in conception and timing to the information we secretly obtain through these intercepted codes."

Marshall was begging Tom Dewey to keep silent for the sake of national security. Remember, in 1944 we were still at war.

But for the moment, at least, Dewey could think only of Roosevelt's role in the secrecy. In the presence of Marshall's messenger, Dewey blurted out, "He knew what was happening before Pearl Harbor! Instead of being reelected, he ought to be impeached!"

And so was Tom Dewey confronted with perhaps the most agonizing decision of his lifetime. Disclose the damning information, ruin Roosevelt, win the election, and tip our hand to Japan—or keep quiet, lose the election, and preserve the state of our national defense.

You know Tom Dewey lost in 1944.

Not only did he keep his mouth shut during the campaign, he *never* revealed his knowledge of the broken Japanese code.

Tom Dewey has been dead for over a decade.

In 1981 a secret document was declassified, a document revealing something Tom Dewey never knew. The Japanese code we cracked back in 1941 was *diplomatic code*, not military code. It was only after the Japanese had attacked Pearl Harbor that U.S. Intelligence learned how to eavesdrop on Japan's military plans.

According to that recently declassified document, FDR had no advance knowledge of the Pearl Harbor attack. Neither, in fact, had Japan's own premier, nor that nation's own minister of war!

Tom Dewey may have gone to his grave wondering whether he had done the right thing.

You know he did. Because now you know THE REST OF THE STORY.

92. Sofie's Share

How do you feel about "palimony"? To what extent are live-in lovers financially responsible for each other?

Sofie and Al lived together off and on for eighteen years. They talked about getting married—really, legally married—but never did.

And then Al died. Rich.

No mention of Sofie in his will.

The year before Al's death, Sofie had broken his heart by marrying another man. Still, Sofie, through her lawyer, met with the executors of Al's will, demanding her "fair share" of her former lover's millions.

Come on, you say, there has to be more to it than that! There is. This is THE REST OF THE STORY.

Al had a weakness for Austrian women. First it was an idealistic Austrian countess. She married someone else. Al rebounded to Sofie, Austrian as well, but a flower girl twenty-three years younger than he.

In a colloquialism yet to be invented, Sofie's porch lights were on, but nobody was home. She was a fun-loving although not quite bright young lady, a voracious consumer of and believer in cheap novels.

Naively, vainly, Al tried to improve Sofie's mind. When that didn't work, he lavished money and finery on the girl. Classically passion-blind, Al was cruising for a bruising. The biggest blow came after almost two decades of emotional turbulence: Sofie was pregnant.

The situation would have been considerably easier to accept had Al been the father. The father was, in this case, a Hungarian aristocrat and cavalry officer.

Sofie's relationship with this dashing young captain was pure soap opera material. He married her and abandoned her the same day. Then he became a champagne salesman. Then he killed himself.

All the while, lonely, lovesick Al continued to send Sofie money. Virtually until his death.

The executors of his estate were most alarmed when they heard from Sofie's attorney. Could Sofie provide proof of her alleged intimate eighteen-year liaison with the deceased?

Yes, she could. In fact, she had saved all the letters Al had ever written to her. Two hundred sixteen letters. And the envelopes, many of which playfully addressed her as "Madame" with Al's surname and in Al's own handwriting.

By this evidence Sofie's lawyer claimed "common-law wife," and thereby the right to inherit Al's fortune. Sofie's true leverage, however, was the threat of scandal. She had already secured a publisher, she said, who was most interested in the prospect of sharing Al's letters with the world.

In the end a scandal was avoided. And the out-of-court settlement set up Sofie for life.

Al's estate would pick up the tab for all attorneys' fees, would provide Sofie with an annual income. In return, Sofie would be required to hand over all of Al's correspondence and, of course, refrain from any act which might harm Al's memory.

Those secrets were among the world's best kept for many years. Almost a century later they are legally relevant. Their true significance is this. . . .

Sofie might have cut even deeper into Al's fortune. Had she done so, all of us would have been poorer. For Al willed his money, or more precisely the ongoing interest from his estate, to each year's outstanding contributors in the fields of physics and chemistry and medicine and literature and international peace.

The fortune which Sofie's posthumous palimony might have drained dry—was that which continues to nourish the annual prizes bearing the name of the man who loved her, Alfred *Nobel*.

93. The Secret Scars

IT HAS BEEN SAID THAT if ever there were an ideal relationship in this far-from-flawless world, it was that of Henry and Frances.

He was a Harvard professor and she was his bride.

Oliver Wendell Holmes was a Cambridge neighbor of theirs. In the summer of 1861 he passed their house, later saying that he had "trembled to look at it," feeling that "those who lived there had their happiness so perfect that no change . . . could fail to be for the worse."

It was as though Holmes had had a premonition of THE REST OF THE STORY.

On the afternoon of July 9, Henry was home napping in his study; Frances was in the adjoining library, putting away keepsakes. She was wrapping locks of her two younger daughters' hair in small paper packages, sealing the packages with wax.

No one knows precisely how it happened. Presumably a breeze from the open library window blew burning wax on Frances' light summer dress. In any event her clothing caught fire, and in moments she was engulfed in flames.

Terrified, Frances ran into the study, screaming for help.

Henry sprang to his feet. There was a small rug on the floor. Henry grabbed it, wrapped it around his wife. But the rug was too small to extinguish the fire.

Frances broke free and ran for the door in panic, then in her confusion spun about and rushed into Henry's arms.

It was Henry's embrace which ultimately smothered

the blaze. Yet for Frances hope was all but gone. Horribly burned, she was carried to her room. A doctor was summoned and soon arrived. By then Frances was suffering unbearably.

Couldn't something be done, Henry demanded?

Mercifully, yes. The physician administered ether. Frances slept. Awakening hours later, she remained awake the rest of the night. In the morning she asked for coffee but shortly thereafter lapsed into a coma from which she would never recover.

That day was her last on earth.

Frances was buried nearby at Mount Auburn, on the thirteenth of July. Her eighteenth wedding anniversary.

Henry, whose own hands and face were dreadfully burned in his attempt to save Frances, was confined to his bed, delirious, unable to attend the funeral.

And long after the physical agony had subsided and the wounds had healed, the weight of remorse lingered on Henry's heart. His was an "unparalleled bereavement," friends observed. Yet even though most of him had died with his beloved, some of him went on living for two decades more and lived to pen the lines which would enchant each generation since:

> Listen, my children, and you shall hear
> Of the midnight ride of Paul Revere . . .

History records that poet Henry Wadsworth Longfellow grew the full beard for which he would always be remembered because of permanent facial scars he sustained at the age of fifty-four—in a fire.

You recall the picture of a full-bearded Longfellow on the classroom wall.

You never saw him without that beard.

Now you know why.

Now you know THE REST OF THE STORY.

94. Kingdom in a File Drawer

FRANK'S EARLY CHILDHOOD was a glorious real-life fantasy. His father had been an oil baron, had amassed a fortune. Now Dad was a gentleman farmer, and the family was living in luxury.

Their home was a sprawling country estate near Syracuse, New York, an opulent manor surrounded by immaculate gardens and manicured greenery and rolling fields of grain. A splendid property which Frank's mother had christened "Rose Lawn."

Life at Rose Lawn was everything a little boy could wish for: adoring parents, plenty of room to romp and to play. In this way Frank's youth was unmarred by conventional childhood trauma. Until one day.

Frank was exploring his father's grainfields. The boy and his mind were wandering equally happily. All at once he was jolted from his daydreams.

It was a stranger, someone young Frank had never seen before, a figure towering over him, standing rigid, silent, alone.

Frank ran home.

For months thereafter, each night, the same nightmare. He would meet the stranger again in his father's field, and in those dread dreams the stranger would chase him.

And then Frank would wake up.

It seemed an unfair blemish on the boy's otherwise carefree childhood. He was so happy at Rose Lawn. Until bedtime. Then, in slumber, he would walk the open fields once more, only to meet and to be pursued by a nameless, faceless stranger.

What happened after the stranger acquired a name and a face is THE REST OF THE STORY.

Now Frank is a grown man with a family of his own, a wife and four sons.

There's a timid knock at his study door.

His youngsters have brought some neighborhood friends to the house to hear another of daddy's marvelous stories.

With four boys of his own, Daddy has become an adept storyteller. So Daddy reaches into his imagination and into his own childhood, and he begins.

For his eager young listeners, Daddy creates a splendid city: a happy place engulfed in green, far from the clutches of care. Daddy remembers Rose Lawn where he grew up, and his descriptions are vivid.

For the children gathered around him he breathes life into the faceless stranger of his own youthful nightmares. But now the stranger is no longer threatening. He is tame. And he has a face.

One of the youngsters interrupts. What does Daddy call this wonderful kingdom?

Daddy stops. He isn't prepared for this. Quickly, his eyes dart about the room for an indication, a clue, something to call his fantasy land.

His eyes come to rest on the file cabinet in the corner. Without thinking, he speaks what he reads on the lowermost file drawer.

The name is satisfactory to his young audience. It will remain so forever.

One day, Daddy wrote down the story he told—of the carefree metropolis engulfed in green which he called Emerald City, and of the once-sinister stranger he had met in his father's field which in reality had been nothing more than a scarecrow, and of the marvelous fantasy kingdom spontaneously named after a file drawer. The file drawer below A-through-N.

You know.

O-through-Z.

For thus was born to L. Frank Baum the magnificent tale which weaves its web of enchantment about the hearts of children still.

The Wonderful Wizard of Oz.

95. Who Were the "Rough Riders"?

THERE WAS WOODBURY KANE, an Ivy League dandy. And Joe Stevens, the world's greatest polo player. There was Dudley Dean, the famed Harvard quarterback. And Bob Wrenn, the nation's number-one-rated tennis player. Hamilton Fish was there too, former captain of the Columbia crew. There were footballers from Princeton, high-jumpers from Yale, gentlemen huntsmen named Wadsworth and Tiffany, and elegant blue-blooded Englishmen.

You've heard so much about them, and you never knew any of their names.

They were Teddy Roosevelt's "Rough Riders."

In April of 1898 McKinley was president, Teddy Roosevelt was assistant secretary of the navy, and we were at war with Spain.

On Monday the twenty-fifth, it was announced that Teddy would be recruiting for the First U.S. Volunteer Cavalry. By Wednesday, twenty-seven sacks of applications had been received. Twenty-three thousand men, enough for an entire division, all begging Teddy for the opportunity to serve under him.

The formal designation "First U.S. Volunteer Cavalry" was quickly ignored, especially by the newspapers out west. "Teddy's Terrors," newsmen began calling them. And "Teddy's Texas Tarantulas." And "Teddy's Gilded Gang." "Teddy's Cavalry Cowpunchers," "Teddy's Cowboy Contingent," "Roosevelt's Rangers," "Roosevelt's Riotous Rounders." Every imaginable alliteration.

There was only one appellation of which Teddy himself fully approved: "Roosevelt's Rough Riders."

He had used the term himself, as early as 1886. He had said that he longed to lead a troop of "roughriders" into battle. And now he would resign as assistant navy secretary to do so.

You have already met by name some of Roosevelt's Ivy League recruits, aristocratic young gentlemen who arrived for training in San Antonio wearing custom leather boots and shirts from Abercrombie and Fitch. Yet in addition to the eastern college athletes and dandies, there were policemen and coal miners and cowboys. Especially cowboys. They comprised approximately three-fourths of the entire regiment.

Recruits who did not measure up wept openly upon learning that they would be left behind.

The lucky ones, the 560 who remained, were off to fight the Spanish on Cuban soil.

Teddy and his Rough Riders are all most of us remember about the Spanish-American War: Teddy Roosevelt leading the Rough Riders' charge up San Juan Hill.

That battle, it is said, carried Teddy to the White House.

But how many of us know THE REST OF THE STORY?

The actual site of the charge was *Kettle* Hill, not San Juan Hill.

Also, Teddy's Rough Riders were not really Teddy's.

The First U.S. Volunteer Cavalry was actually under the command of Colonel Leonard Wood. Teddy was *second* in command.

And one thing more, when the Rough Riders embarked on the Cuba-bound troopships, they were informed that there would be no room for their horses.

And so Teddy's men actually charged up Kettle Hill *on foot.*

Roosevelt's Rough Riders were neither Roosevelt's nor, throughout the entire Spanish-American War, did they ride!

96. A Christmas Memory

LOCKED AWAY INSIDE each of us is the recollection of a very special holiday. Often it is a scene from childhood, as is this next, a fond Christmas memory of a winter long past.

Charlie was ten.

School was out and it was Christmas vacation. The family would spend their holiday in the country.

A light snow was falling. Charlie pressed his nose against the window glass. How unlike the big city, where traffic blackened the white loveliness almost before it touched the street! Here, all was quiet and cottony white.

How would Charlie like to go out for a car ride in the snow, his mother asked?

Charlie would like that.

So the boy and his mother got into the car and drove off down the snow-laden lane.

Even the tiniest twigs on the barren trees glistened. Charlie wondered what made the ice cling like that. And he listened to the squeaky crunch of the snow under the car tires.

The snow began falling more heavily. A mile or so down the road was a gentle curve. Mother knew it was there, and she drove slowly approaching it. But a patch of ice caused the automobile to slide off to the side and into a shallow snowdrift.

Charlie thought it was fun. Mother smiled and shifted into reverse. No traction; the wheels were spinning. And Mother was no longer smiling.

Charlie would not wait to be asked. He opened the passenger door and climbed down into the snow. "I'll push!" he declared, and he scampered around to the front of the car.

Again Mother stepped on the accelerator. Despite her son's effort to assist, the automobile just sat there, stuck!

It was all right, Mother said, there was a house not far away. Strangers, yet surely friendly. Hand in hand, young Charlie and his mom started walking.

And the snow fell more heavily.

It seemed a very long way up the slippery lane. Then at last, in a vague silhouette against the gray-white sky, the big house loomed before them.

Mother knocked on the door. Moments later it was answered by a lady with a kind face. Yes, of course, Charlie and his mother could come in. Yes, of course, they could use the telephone. And the lady nodded in apparent concern as they related their predicament.

It wasn't long before someone had come to rescue the adventurers, mother and son.

It was a very special holiday.

I realize this happening does not sound extraordinary. Yet to Charlie's mother, and especially to young Charlie, it was an extraordinary occasion.

For during the Christmas season of 1958—in England, at Sandringham—a ten-year-old boy learned what it was like to be ordinary. And that was most remarkable in itself.

For all the pomp and ceremony which has followed him since, there is that one halcyon scene from his childhood, that adventurous afternoon meant only for him and his mother. Neither he nor she would ever forget the look on the face of the kind lady at Anmer Hall, when two visitors came to call.

A mother and son seeking refuge from the snow.

Elizabeth, queen of England, and ten-year-old Charles, heir to the throne!

Now you know THE REST OF THE STORY.

97. Johnny You Hardly Knew Him

WHAT MADE ABE LINCOLN LOOK the way he did—gawky, angular, taller than he really was?

Dr. Harold Schwartz of the University of Southern California believes he knows THE REST OF THE STORY.

Dr. Schwartz is perhaps the world's leading authority on a genetic disorder known as Marfan's syndrome. It affects the body's connective tissue. Dr. Schwartz says President Lincoln had Marfan's, unquestionably. In fact, he has been studying Abe's condition for the past twenty-four years, since 1959.

It is well known that Lincoln's arms, legs, hands, feet were disproportionately long, even for a man of his height. Lincoln himself once observed that there wasn't a lumberjack in Maine "with longer arms than mine."

From the casts of Lincoln hands, sculptors have noted that the first bone in the middle finger is almost half an inch longer than that of most people's hands. Lincoln contemporaries often described the president's legs as "spiderlike." Remarkably, that is the same phrase used in a description of Marfan's syndrome by French physician Bernard-Jean Marfan, for whom the disease is named.

From photographs and casts and contemporary observations and even Lincoln's own words, Dr. Harold Schwartz has become convinced of Abe's condition. Even the habitual squint of Lincoln's left eye, says the doctor, is a symptom of Marfan's.

He first became interested in Lincoln's case in 1959, after examining a young boy with Marfan's syndrome. Dr. Schwartz learned that the child's maternal grandfather also had Marfan's. His last name was Lincoln. Yes, a distant relative of Abe's.

Dr. Schwartz then recalled the detailed descriptions of Lincoln from Sandburg's biography, and suddenly everything fell into place. In the years since, Dr. Schwartz has traced the Lincoln Marfan gene all the way back to England, through four centuries of the Lincoln family tree.

And still more incredible evidence, in 1863 President Lincoln had his picture taken sitting in a chair with his legs crossed, the left leg over the right. Lincoln's left foot, therefore, was suspended above the floor.

When that picture was developed, Lincoln had noticed that his left foot seemed out of focus. Everything else in the picture was sharp, clear. Only Lincoln's left foot was blurry.

The president asked a friend if this imperfection was the photographer's fault. The friend, a fellow named Noah Brooks, said definitely not.

He asked Lincoln to sit in a chair with his legs crossed, as he had for the photograph.

Lincoln sat, crossed his legs. To the president's astonishment his left foot was throbbing, actually moving enough to blur a photographic image!

Dr. Schwartz recognizes this as "aortic regurgitation," which causes a pulse so strong that it can shake the lower part of the leg. The condition is related to Marfan's syndrome.

Just think how history might have changed had John Wilkes Booth known THE REST OF THE STORY. . . .

There is one thing more you ought to know about Marfan's. It is incurable. And the disease or the complications thereof are ultimately fatal.

Dr. Schwartz, determining the degree to which Lincoln's case had advanced, is convinced the president would have been dead within a year. Had he not been assassinated first.

What that says is: John Booth wasted his time and his own life—murdering a dead man!

98. House Calls

In 1961, THE DOCTOR became a patient.

Sixty-eight-year-old Dr. Louis Camuti, hardly sick a day in his life, was suddenly stricken with a condition which not even a physician of his experience could identify.

In a New York hospital, Dr. Camuti's own doctors attempted to diagnose the mysterious illness. There were many tests. Finally, after ten days in the hospital, Dr. Camuti was told THE REST OF THE STORY.

His condition, although to an extent controllable, was incurable. Continuing his practice would seem out of the question.

So Dr. Camuti pondered this medical verdict, and he reflected on his own forty-year medical career. He made up his mind that no matter the discomfort, no matter the threat to his personal health, he would not abandon his own patients. Dr. Camuti's practice would go on.

East side, west side, all around the town, a sigh of relief could be heard. For Dr. Louis Camuti was among the last of his breed, a priceless commodity in an era of depersonalized production-line medicine.

He was a doctor who made house calls.

He had an office, but he spent very little time there. Eight to nine hours a day he was out in the community, in and around New York City, visiting his patients.

Because parking was almost always a problem, Dr. Camuti's wife Alexandra drove him everywhere.

Because the doctor believed so strongly that a patient is

better off convalescing in his or her home, Dr. Camuti often performed minor surgery—while on a house call! Sterile operating rooms for complex surgery, of course. Yet quite often Dr. Camuti operated on patients in their private residences!

After four decades of cultivating unequivocal trust, the good doctor had become somewhat of a Manhattan legend. So many depended upon him. Even though his medical condition had given him every reason in the world to retire, he would not desert those who needed him.

So Dr. Camuti left the hospital to continue his practice.

As before, wife Alexandra would chauffeur his daily rounds, and when possible the doctor would operate in the homes of his patients.

The telephone calls continued in the middle of the night, from rich and poor, from teachers and lawyers and shopkeepers and celebrities.

One urgent telegram, a house-call request, almost put Dr. Camuti on an airplance bound for Naples, Italy!

He would remain active for another two decades, extending his extraordinary practice to sixty years. Then, in February of 1981, Dr. Camuti passed away. A heart attack en route to a house call. He was eighty-seven.

As far as we know, the medical condition originally diagnosed in 1961 had played no part in his death, although it made his last twenty years particularly difficult.

For Dr. Camuti's patients, the Manhattanite recipients of his remarkable bedside manner, were cats. Dr. Camuti was a doctor of *veterinary* medicine, specializing in cats. He was perhaps the world's best-known, best-loved *cat* doctor.

And the condition which hospitalized him in 1961, the affliction under which he lovingly labored all through the last two decades of his unique house-call practice, had been a severe allergy—*to cats.*

99. Ralph Neves, DOA

IT IS MAY 8, 1936, and you are alone in the basement of Crosby's Mortuary near Burlingame, California.

Well, you're not quite alone.

On a slab, awaiting preparations for funeral and burial, is a body with an identification tag on its toe. The body of a young man named Ralph Neves.

Ralph is wearing his pants and one boot, and that's it. As though he were just dumped there quickly, carelessly.

He was.

Ralph Neves was an eighteen-year-old jockey. On the afternoon of May 8, he was racing at Bay Meadows in San Mateo.

It happened in the fourth race. Ralph was running fourth place. Thundering into the fast turn out of the backstretch, Ralph's mount stumbled. Five horses came down in the jam-up. Ralph was catapulted high in the air. When the trampling hooves were silent and the dust had settled, there was Ralph, lying in the track, motionless.

Three doctors rushed to the scene as thousands of spectators murmured anxiously. Jockey Neves was pronounced dead even before the stretcher arrived. Minutes later, his body was placed in an ambulance and driven to a nearby hospital.

But the hospital did not want Ralph Neves.

"Don't waste our time," the ambulance driver was told; "take him straight to Crosby's Mortuary."

That's how Ralph wound up in Crosby's basement with

nothing on but his pants and one boot. The ambulance driver simply deposited him and left.

When Ralph's friend Horace Wald heard what had happened, he hurried to the mortuary. At first the mortician was reluctant to allow Horace to see Ralph. Then Horace explained that he was a doctor, was used to such things.

Lucky for Ralph that Horace was a physician.

For when Dr. Wald was taken downstairs, he gazed at Jockey Ralph Neves for a long time. And then suddenly, inexplicably, he was compelled to reach out and touch Ralph's neck to feel for a pulse. And there was a pulse! A faint pulse, but a pulse!

Dr. Wald ran out to his car, returned with his black bag. A single shot of adrenaline brought Ralph bolt-upright on the slab, and before Dr. Wald could say a word the jockey had fled the mortuary in panic.

Ralph ran two miles to San Mateo, then hailed a cab. Still frightened and confused, he demanded, "Take me to Bay Meadows track!" The driver took him to Bay Meadows.

Before the cab had stopped at the curb, Ralph jumped out—still wearing only his pants and one boot—and ran into the grandstand. Someone cried, "That's Ralph Neves, the dead jockey!"

There were screams. The crowd started chasing him. Ralph kept running. And he didn't stop until he dropped from exhaustion.

The next day, May 9, Ralph was back in the saddle, back on the track and racing. He continued to ride until he retired, twenty-eight years later.

One of the doctors who had pronounced him dead just shook his head. A "profound depression of the nervous system," he called it. That's what had made it seem Ralph Neves had died.

The only reason I bring any of this to your attention is that one of these days you'll be reading a roster of the Racing-Hall-of-Famers, and you'll see the name of Ralph Neves, 3,772 first finishes—the fourteenth winningest jockey of all time!

And you'll know that in order to establish that record, Ralph almost had to come back from the grave. Because now you know THE REST OF THE STORY.

100. The Outcasts

IF THERE IS A STAIN on the record of our forefathers, one dark hour in the earliest history of the American colonies, it would be the hanging of the so-called "witches" at Salem.

But that was a pinpoint in place and time, a brief lapse into hysteria.

For the most part, our seventeenth-century colonists were scrupulously fair, even in fear.

There was one group of people they feared with reason— a society, you might say, whose often insidious craft had claimed a multitude of victims, ever since the Middle Ages in Europe.

One group of people, hated and feared from Massachusetts Bay to Virginia.

The magistrates would not burn them at the stake, although surely a great many of the colonists might have recommended such a solution.

Our forefathers were baffled by them.

In the first place, where did they come from? Of all who sailed from England to Plymouth in 1620, not one of those two-legged vermin was aboard.

"Vermin."

That's what the colonists called them.

Parasites who fed on human misery, spreading sorrow and confusion wherever they went.

"Destructive," they were called.

And still they were permitted coexistence with the colonists

For a while, anyway.

Of course, there were colonial laws prohibiting the practice of their infamous craft. Somehow a way was always found around those laws.

In 1641, Massachusetts Bay colony took a novel approach to the problem. The governors attempted to starve those "devils" out of existence through economic exclusion. They were denied wages, and thereby it was hoped that they would perish.

Four years later Virginia followed the example of Massachusetts Bay, and for a while it seemed that the dilemma had been resolved.

It had not.

Somehow the parasites managed to survive, and the mere nearness of them made the colonists' skin crawl.

In 1658 in Virginia the final solution:

Banishment.

Exile.

The "treacherous ones" were cast out of the colony.

At last, after decades of enduring the psychological gloom, the sun came out and the birds sang and all was right with the world. And the elation continued for a generation.

I'm not sure why the Virginians eventually allowed the outcasts to return, but they did.

In 1680, after twenty-two years, the despised ones were readmitted to the colony on the condition that they be subjected to the strictest surveillance.

How soon we forget.

For indeed, over the next half-century or so, the imposed restrictions were slowly, quietly swept away. And those whose treachery had been feared since the Middle Ages ultimately took their place in society.

You see, the "vermin" that once infested colonial America, the parasites who preyed on the misfortune of their neighbors until finally they were officially banished from Virginia, those dreaded, despised, and inevitably outcast masters of confusion were *lawyers*.

Now you know THE REST OF THE STORY.

101. The Saga of Admiral Ivan Pavel

FEW COMMANDERS WHO ever sailed for the Russian Navy possessed the greatness of Admiral Ivan Pavel. He won many battles at sea. Toward the end of the eighteenth century he rescued Kherson and the Crimea from the Turks.

To this day, the Russians barely acknowledge his accomplishments. And this is THE REST OF THE STORY.

Ivan himself once described Russia under Catherine the Great as a country of "the dark intrigues and mean subterfuges of Asiatic jealousy and malice."

He had already proved himself as a superior naval commander. But when the empress called him to Saint Petersburg to propose his participation in a new war, he was at first reticent. He feared not the treachery of the Turks, but that of his own comrades in arms.

Friends begged him to reconsider. Ivan was born to lead a fleet of ships into battle, they said. So Ivan reconsidered and hurried to Saint Petersburg, to the court of Catherine II.

That was in April 1788.

The empress was most charming. She flattered Ivan, promised him supreme command in the campaign against the Turks. Ivan accepted enthusiastically, and the newly commissioned rear admiral was dispatched to the Black Sea.

As it developed, Ivan's command was not quite supreme. His superior, with the blessings of the empress herself, was the treacherous and unbalanced Grigori Potëmkin.

Ivan's colleague, another of Catherine's puppets, was the arrogant and cowardly Prince Charles Nassau-Siegen.

And yet even with his associates quickly becoming his adversaries, Admiral Ivan behaved admirably, ignoring their deceit. "The first duty of a gentleman," Ivan wrote, "is to respect his own character."

Ivan's naval victories in the Black Sea were stunning. As you already know, the Russians' triumph over the Turks was mainly the triumph of Admiral Ivan.

But Russian history does not read quite that way. For while Ivan won the battles—and historically there can be no doubt of that—others took the credit!

All the while behind the scenes, the empress encouraged subordinates to dispute Ivan's authority. He became the object of every imaginable conspiracy. Finally, in March of 1789, after Ivan had returned to Saint Petersburg, he was falsely accused of assaulting a young girl. Apparently Catherine was behind that too.

Shortly thereafter Ivan left Russia, disillusioned, embittered, and traveled to France. His health failed rapidly, and he died in Paris in July of 1792.

He had recognized the "dark intrigues" of Russia under Catherine the Great. Still, he had allowed friends like Thomas Jefferson to talk him into the Russian Navy. A diplomatic move that misfired.

Ivan was not Russian. He was American. An incomparable naval officer in our own Revolutionary War.

During that war he had never risen above the rank of captain.

In fact, when he died in Paris, he was buried in an unmarked grave in Saint Louis Cemetery for Protestants. For more than a hundred years, no one even knew he was there.

Admiral Ivan Pavel of the Russian Navy.

Ivan: John.

Pavel: Paul.

John Paul Jones.

102. Gem of the Mountains

IT WAS THE PROSPECT of gold which brought people into the territory in the first place. Those who came decided to stay.

By February of 1859, an act had been introduced in Congress which would make that chunk of land spanning the Rockies an official U.S. territory. The name "Osage Territory" was proposed. Yet there was too much congressional foot-dragging to suit the enthusiastic inhabitants of the area. And so on June 6 a constitutional convention assembled, and the name "Jefferson Territory" was adopted. Then the election of a delegate to Congress was scheduled.

Had duly elected delegate B. D. Williams simply gone to Washington, D. C., and gained the acceptance of Jefferson Territory as an official territory of the United States, the eventual state would have been called Jefferson. Of course, there is no such state, and here's why.

Among the unsuccessful candidates for territorial delegate was a fellow named George M. Willing. He decided to go to Washington anyway, and he met delegate Williams there. He told delegate Williams that Congress would be unlikely to buy the name Jefferson for the new territory, and that he, George Willing, had a better name: Idaho. It was an Indian word, George said. It meant "gem of the mountains."

Delegate Williams said that Idaho was a very nice name indeed, but that the territorial inhabitants had already chosen "Jefferson," and "Jefferson" they would get.

Shortly thereafter, both House and Senate committees determined that to start a trend of naming territories after presidents would not be a good idea, and that President Washington's should remain a singular honor.

So what about the name Idaho, George Willing once more asked? Delegate Williams replied that if "Jefferson" was out of the question, a number of names should be pondered and carefully evaluated.

Names proposed to the Senate committee included "Tampa" and "Nemara" and "Weapollao" and "Arapahoe" and even "San Juan." The House committee seemed particularly fond of "Tahosa," an Indian word meaning "dwellers on the mountaintops."

The names of Columbus, Franklin, and Lafayette were also considered for the new territory. But the one name, apparently irresistible to all, was George Willing's original suggestion: Idaho. "Gem of the mountains." What could be more appropriate? But this is THE REST OF THE STORY.

Delegate B. D. Williams, still suspicious of territorial tagalong George Willing, decided to research the origin of the Indian word "Idaho." He discovered not only that Idaho did *not* mean "gem of the mountains," but that Idaho had no meaning at all.

There was no such word, in *any* language, as "Idaho"!

Suddenly realizing that the Idaho proposal had been George Willing's practical joke from the start, delegate Williams hurried back to the Hill with this warning: The name Idaho was a fake. It meant nothing, least of all "gem of the mountains." That the name of a territory and ultimately a state should be the product of a practical joker's imagination was unthinkable. Therefore, the new territory must receive another name. A *legitimate* name.

And it did.

The name "Idaho" was abandoned.

And on February 8, 1861, *Colorado* was born.

103. The Kingdom of Love

THE ROYAL EDICT was proclaimed near and far. The young prince, who would soon ascend to the throne, was seeking a suitable princess. All the noble families of the kingdom must escort their eligible daughters to the court, for from among them the future queen would be chosen.

It is said that two thousand highborn young ladies were brought before the prince, and that he was attracted to only one.

Many had come from nobler families. Others might have made a more politically advantageous marriage. Yet for the young prince there was an even higher consideration: He had fallen in love.

It sounds like the setting of a fairy tale. But it happened just that way, once upon a time, more than four hundred years ago.

It was the beginning of a real-life love story history almost forgot. And this is THE REST OF THE STORY.

In 1547, the young prince was crowned king. Shortly thereafter, he made the girl of his dreams his queen.

I know of no royal romance quite like it. For the benevolence of this young monarch's reign was directly reflective of his profoundly affectionate marital relationship. It was as though the youthful king and queen, as a result of their devotion to each other, set out to transform their country into a kingdom of love:

There began a new era in that nation's history, one in which the king was regarded as a father to his subjects and in which those subjects were restored to equanimity. A traveler in that land wrote home, "I think no prince in Christendom is better beloved."

In the goverment's high council, members were free to express any opinion no matter how contrary to the king's.

For the first time ever in that nation, its poorest citizen had access through petition to its leader. Indeed, the king became a particular friend of the poor, a humanitarian devoted to charity and to the relief of suffering everywhere.

The king proved to be a godly man, a builder of churches, a humble ruler who fasted and prayed, a monarch who believed that the men in his government should be good men, and that the children of his kingdom should be set early upon the paths of righteousness.

To all such things which were good, the queen encouraged her king. It was her tenderness which had tamed the raucous boy and urged him into a manhood of dignity. It was her virtue which had inspired his godliness, her benevolence and understanding which had served as moral examples for the wisest leader that nation had ever followed. In turn, he, the king, loved her, his queen, as few men who have ever lived have ever loved.

And then one day, the queen fell ill. The king frantically summoned his finest medical advisers. The king wept. The king prayed. The queen died.

And the king changed.

The fairy tale was finished. A nightmare was only beginning.

For once upon a time, there was a king who threw himself into a life of dissipation and drunken revelry, who seized those who had been his friends and tortured them and impaled them on stakes and burned them alive, a sadistic beast of a man who murdered children, even his own.

History almost forgot the saint he was, remembering instead the demon he became. For after thirteen years of glory and goodness, that nation's most benevolent ruler became its most evil. His mind, twisted by grief and determined to destroy the haunting memories, became in its torment the supreme instrument of destruction.

But don't let it be forgot—that the kingdom bathed in blood was once wrapped in dreams. And that the king, more than a king, the czar of all Russia, with his bride by his side was Ivan the Wonderful.

Only when she, Anastasia, was gone—when the light in the czar's heart was extinguished forever—the fiend that remained was *Ivan the Terrible.*